14 Sep 05

~~For~~ HANG-UPS!

Mary Lou

warm
wishes—
Gloria
Heidi

D1052647

HANG-UPS!

The Secret Life
of Clothes

Gloria Heidi

TUDOR HALL PRESS

Cover Design: Amity Press
Cover Photograph: Tom Thompson Photography
Text Design: Val Sherer

Library of Congress Control Number: 2002115745
ISBN 0-9654172-7-1

Third Printing: March, 2005
Printed in the United States of America
Published by arrangement with
Tudor Hall Press
Greenbrae, California

For Bob

who makes so many
wonderful things possible

Other Books by Gloria Heidi

- *Winning the Age Game*
  (Doubleday)

- *New Beginnings: Cosmetic Surgery*
  for Men and Women
  (Doubleday)

- *Close-Up: Gloria Heidi's Ten Day*
  Makeover Plan (G.P. Putnam's Sons)

- *Face-Up! An Easy Exercise System*
  to Firm, Tone and Recontour Your Face
  (Cannon Publishing)

Television Productions

- *Image: Projections of Identity*
  (Documentary/P.B.S.)

- *Gloria Heidi's Close-Up Adventure*
  (Cannon Productions)

Contents

Prologue

Prologue

I opened The Closet Door, stepped inside, and made a fascinating discovery. The clothes that hang there, so silent, so passive, are not mere backdrops to the drama of our lives. No. These costumes have a life of their own and they influence the unfolding events in ours.

They've shared your secrets. Now you can learn theirs — and the hidden agendas which affect you in profound ways.

As every woman knows, a secret has little value if you keep it to yourself. So, if you'll move your chair just a little bit closer, I'll tell you some of those secrets now...

1

Out
of the
Closet

Out of the Closet

*I*n this era of "Enquiring minds want to know", a time when liaisons of all kinds have been revealed to the gossip hungry public, there's one intimate relationship that remains unexamined. Yet it's an emotional attraction that almost everyone has experienced, even the most proper among us.

This particular relationship, so fascinating, so fulfilling, so satisfying, has been a lifelong passion of mine. (And I know I'm not alone in this proclivity, as you shall see.)

So I'm going to tell you the inside story. Fearlessly. Hang the consequences.

Some of my best friends are clothes! (And to tell the truth, there's a certain red dress from my past that I absolutely *adored*.)

Yes. It's true. I admit it. But before you say, "Get a life!!! Get out there and meet some *people*!", let me explain.

The truth is, our clothes are among our most intimate and close companions. Usually friends, sometimes enemies, they play an influential role in the drama of our lives.

If we are wise, knowledgeable, or creative, our clothes are strong supportive friends, giving us courage where none may have existed before.

Is there a woman alive who doesn't have at least one memory of finding ("Thank you, God — and Macy's") that perfect dress for some crucial event in her life? Remembering, we can see that this dress had all the qualities of a true friend, revealing our best qualities, making light of our faults, and championing our cause to strangers.

Of course, clothes can be cruel enemies, too. (And you may have your own painful memory of an event when you were wearing the absolutely *wrong*, Oh-So-Wrong thing.) Yes, foolish, naive choices in costume can betray us as neatly as any false love. Call in the paparazzi, and I'll show them that in love or war, "dressed to kill" can apply to seductress or soldier.

True, many of our most memorable experiences are played out without any clothes at all. But usually, unless one's romantic interludes occur on some swinging nudist isle in the Caribbean, our clothes have been the supporting cast in our romantic plays. And, as every actor knows, there are no small parts. Each carefully chosen, seductive detail contributes to the ensemble Big Finish.

These costars play their parts well; the tiny, ingénue bow, tying a strategic strap (just pull the ribbon and, *voila!*); the gamin sweater whose clinging fit reveals the subtle outline of breast and nipple; the bias ruffle at the hem of a black chiffon cocktail dress (perhaps sprayed with perfume to create a background chorus of evocative scent). Like a group of avid, matchmaking relatives, they do their best to help the romance along.

And who's to say that these costumes don't, in some way, share our romantic interludes?

Perhaps, when they are put away after being properly buttoned, buckled, and zipped, they gossip and reminisce about their adventures. Perhaps it is thrilling to them, after primly hanging in the closet, after being part of the careful and calculated preparation for a Big Evening, to be suddenly removed with passionate abandon — his evening trousers crumpled on the floor beside the bed, the tie and shirt flung into a corner — her dress in a silky pool beside the chaise, satin sandals topsy-turvy, earrings and rings in a glittering tumble on the bedside table. Stockings and panties are morning-after discoveries. "… now, how in the world did these end-up under the sofa cushions?"

Not all of our clothes are gadabout, Victoria's Secret wannabes. There are the really close friends who are indispensable to one's survival. You know the ones I mean.

The cozy shapeless sweat suit. The mammoth fuzzy slippers.

Or the motherly terry-cloth or chenille robe, frayed at the collar and cuffs, soft and faded, undemanding. (No need to hold in one's stomach.) This is a perfect, Central Casting maternal type. Such a robe is the ideal companion for those bleak times when all you can manage is to curl-up in front of the TV, with a pint of French vanilla Haägen-Daz (to be spooned out of the carton) and "The Way We Were"[1] on the VCR.

The enveloping warmth of a friendly old robe almost whispers, "There, there, it'll be all right." And it's true. After a time you dry your tears, cinch-in the sash, perhaps rally your energies enough to give yourself a facial. And you survive!

The Really Good Black Suit is another trusty ally. A strong supporting player, this clothing companion is like a loving and wise Big Sister and gives you courage in the offices of divorce lawyers and in interviews with unsympathetic personnel officers. At funerals, the Really Good Black Suit stands with you, helping you to bear up and present a dignified demeanor to grieving friends and feuding, dysfunctional family.

Still, friendships don't always last forever. Sadly, just as with our human friends, we occasionally have to reevaluate our clothing relationships.

Clothes, like people, have to carry their weight, contribute something. They can't be idle hangers-on, crowding the closet, sending out negative vibes, making things uncomfortable for our really active relationships. At some point, they have to go, these old friends who have not progressed, who are part of the past and no longer fit-in. Or perhaps they are just old, and can no-longer keep-up with a really active life.

But what to do with these old friends? I hate to bundle them up, stuff them into a brown paper bag, and hustle them along to the indignity of some charity drive. I like to think of an old clothing friend as going on to a new life and new adventures. So I usually try to place my special favorites in one of those pseudo-chic resale shops, imagining them posing smartly in the store's display window. With these good intentions, I regularly go through a predictable little ritual which, ultimately, is as humiliating to me as it is to my clothes.

Newly pressed, clinging to padded hangers, my clothing friends (like aristocrats in the tumbrel) take that long last ride to *Second Hand Rose: Twice Told Fashions*.

The proprietors of these second-time around shops are invariably more demanding than any appraiser at Sotheby's. "We take only new, up-to-the-minute clothes," the haughty manager will say with a disdainful air as she rejects my darlings. But a quick look around at the current stock in one of these shops tells a different story. I mean, I recognize those flowered Carole Little lounging pajamas as *really* old, not quite vintage, an embarrassing relic from the Eighties. That yellowing white flannel suit is not only old, but elementally unflattering — the Bergdorf Goodman label doesn't change that.

It's all very confusing. If all the clothes were truly "like new" and "never worn," why would we want to sell them? But then, the answer becomes obvious. The stock in most of these shops would seem to be composed of those shopping disasters that we all experience. "I must have been out of my mind…" we mutter as we safety-pin the Sak's tag back onto the sleeve of the pink-orange-and-peagreen plaid suit that will eventually "make the cut" at our local Reprise Shoppe.

By contrast, the used clothing of the rich and royal, the famous and infamous, has no trouble at all in being accepted for second time around revivals in the form of much publicized auctions and museum exhibits. These events create a sort of resurrection for an item of used clothing, infusing the garment itself with all the charisma and glamour of a celebrated life.

We see this in the auctioning of Marilyn Monroe's beaded gown, the notorious "Happy Birthday, Mr. President" costume. Widely covered by the media, this event was a grand production and presented an *All About Eve* scenario.[2] The understudy gown, alone in the spotlight at last, became a star.

The sale of Elvis Presley's opulent costumes tells another story, demonstrating so clearly his cosmic destiny. Like a matador dancing with death in the arena, he wore the ritual Suit of Lights. In retrospect, we can sense that he was, indeed, a sort of Dionesian offering. Deprived of a normal life, he was destined to be sacrificed in the coliseum of public obsession. One might paraphrase Shakespeare, "Whom the god's would destroy, they first make famous."

The French have always recognized clothing as a dynamic aspect of life and have devoted several museums to the subject. On every trip to Paris, I include a pilgrimage to the extraordinary *Musée de la Mode et du Textile*. Have you been there? Then you'll remember that, unlike most museums, it's not at all cold and scholarly. Rather, it is the perfect stage setting for its subject matter.

On my most recent tour of the *Musée*, I gained new insight into the power and influence of costume — a sort of revelation that I want to share with you...

It can be hot in Paris in August, and it felt good to leave the sweltering street. I stepped into the cool marble foyer of the museum and went up the wide stairs to the galleries.

It was very quiet and almost deserted, a rare event in this busy season. A young couple and a family of tourists walked past me and then I had the place to myself.

As I moved into the main hall, I caught my breath. The scene that met my eyes was so magical, I felt as if I had somehow been transported into a Cocteau dream sequence. The curators had outdone themselves. In the darkened gallery, each display case had been swathed, floor to ceiling, in filmy drap-

eries. They were lit from within so that each glass case glowed with a soft light, like a huge Japanese lantern at a giant's summer dance.

Mysterious and inscrutable behind the sheer curtains, the silhouetted mannequins posed, waiting seductively for the viewer to pull back the veil for a closer look.

I strolled through the hushed galleries and viewed the intriguing exhibits. As I studied the magnificent creations behind the glass, I became aware more than ever of the influential role that clothes — no, let's call them what they are — "costumes", play in life's dramas. And it was obvious that these costumes had been involved in very high drama indeed.

Some of these stories are well known. The saga of the Duchess of Windsor, for example, whose gowns occupied a prominent position in the gallery.

The stilted museum notes have left out the best part of her story. I recalled that she was the unlikely enchantress (back in the Thirties) who enthralled Edward VIII, King of England. He wanted to make her his wife and queen. When his Ministers (and his mother!) said: "No way!", he gave up the throne. Imagine!

"I cannot go on…without the woman I love," he proclaimed in a dramatic radio address. And they eloped to a chateau on the outskirts of Paris. (It was all very Noel Coward.) They married and thus became the Romantic Windsors and she the quintessential duchess.

The display of gowns designed for the demanding Duchess by Christian Dior was especially impressive. These were as opulent as those of an empress, befitting a would-be queen. There was a robe manteau (a weighty evening wrap) that had all the implications of a royal robe. Dramatically severe, it was fashioned of silken brocade and encrusted with a thousand paillettes, pearls, and jewels. I could imagine the Duchess, jewels reflecting up onto her small cruel face, making an arrogant entrance at a Venetian Ball. The costume clearly says, "Who needs to be a frumpy queen when you can be a Byzantine empress!"

There were other players, less well-known, but nevertheless grande dames — their wardrobes a backup chorus line for spectacular lives. I met (through the brief biography in the display case) Cléopatre-Diane de Mérode (1875-1960), daughter of baronne de Mérode, marquise de Trélon, descendent of comtes de Berchtoldt, etc., etc. Celebrated in Europe and the United States for her beauty, she was known as "the most beautiful woman in the world."

She was a woman worthy of kings, no doubt about it. Her lovers were rumored to be Alphonse XIII of Spain, Léopold of Belgium and Edward VII of England.

I could easily believe all this as I viewed the luxurious gowns and wraps behind the glass. Her beauty still lived in the silvery, shimmering robe du soir that was admiring itself in a strategically-positioned dressing mirror. The twenty-inch waist, captured forever in the reflection, had outwitted time and cuisine.

Then there was Madeline Dittenhover, a rare American player in this ensemble (1889-1969). She was the daughter of Samuel Dittenhover, who established the five-and-ten-cent store concept throughout Europe with Midas-like results. (They were very rich.) La Dittenhover divided her time (so the gallery notes said) between Claridge's in London and the Hotel Bristol in Paris, each seasonal pilgrimage accompanied by mountains of luggage.

Described as arrogant and obstinate, her large, sweeping tri-cornered hats told of a headstrong, demanding personality. She must have been a tartar (there was no mistaking those hats!) because, though a major client of Lanvin, Molyneaux, and Pacquin, even the brief bio revealed that she tried the patience of all she encountered.

But enough of this literal tittle-tattle! I had overtaxed my fragile French vocabulary, attempting to translate each sartorial detail in the museum notes. The dreamlike mood of the gallery inspired my own sense of theatre and as I moved to the more contemporary fashions, I simply looked, and allowed the clothes to tell me their secrets.

The glamourous costumes of comtesse du Z— for example. What were they whispering? Well, she must have been a real bombshell, back there in the Forties, judging from the shapely mannequins who displayed her gowns. Knowing nothing at all about her, I speculated and noted the exotic luxury and extreme décolletage of her wardrobe. Was she perhaps a social upstart? A mistress who finally made the grade to respectable — and impressive — matrimony?

Maybe she wore that elaborate violet outfit at Longchamp, in her first defiant appearance as a legitimate countess. And when did she wear that severely tailored (but still provocative) black silk suit? Was it chosen to favorably influence the prenuptial agreement, to be signed in the intimidating offices of the old Count's legal advisors? Or perhaps, when the Count died, she had worn this suit at the funeral, hoping to catch the eye of another benefactor.

The dresses and suits of baronne de D — told another story. She must have been tall. And what shall I say? Sturdy. The delicate chiffons and intricate, fussy tailoring of the Thirties seemed to emphasize the stolid silhouette that even the compliant mannequins could not disguise. One dress was especially touching. Its chronology in the collection would indicate that the Baronne had moved into "a certain age" (that gentle French description of the over-forty woman). Behind the glass I saw a girlish, flowered pastel day dress, unsuitable (even at this distance) for a substantial size fourteen matron.

One could imagine the Baronne's indecision as she looked at her reflection in the mirrored atelier of her favorite designer. "Is this gown perhaps too young for me? Will he look at me again with desire?" Of course, anyone could see that it was the wrong choice. No supportive clothing friend, this ingénue gown seemed to me to be a cruel sycophant, snickering behind her back.

I wondered about the rest of her story as I continued to wander through the galleries. The Baronne's misstep seemed unique in the collection. (Had she been shopping with an envious "friend" — a potential rival? "Ma chere, c'est vous!")

Most of the spectacular gowns, coats, hats, wraps, shawls and evening finery seemed to be totally effective in their alchemy. While some of the original owners may have been beautiful, no doubt others were just pretty or even plain. No matter. These exalted costumes had power. Under their transforming spell, even downright unattractive women could become stunning, fascinating beauties.

No wonder the Very Rich have such an air, I thought. It struck me that these remarkable costumes were not so much friends as courtiers, constantly reinforcing the wearer's sense of importance and social position, whispering to each woman that she was beautiful, special, desirable. And every sartorial compliment would be escalated with flattering "asides" from the brilliant accessories, which were spotlighted in their own displays.

There were no plastic combs or Lauder giveaway bags here. Rather, I saw extravagant baubles — delicate tortoise shell combs in clever designs, cunningly fashioned chamois gloves, witty hats, Baroque compacts. Combs, brushes, mirrors, tiny purses — one could only imagine the perfume. And there were sleek alligator train cases, each one complete with heavy sterling and crystal fittings, ready to board the Orient Express.

I had come to the last exhibit. I turned and looked back through the galleries, at the showcases with their softly glowing lantern shows — at the mannequin divas, ever ready for their next performance.

Suddenly, I had such a sense of the life force captured in each of the extraordinary costumes displayed there. They had participated in so many scenes, were witness to countless outcomes and events. And no doubt, they had often made a major contribution to the lives of the people who had worn them.

A rush of energy seemed to fill the hall and, in a series of quick movie-like clips, I saw a montage of the scenes that each of these remarkable costumes had shared. It was a bright pageant of impossibly grand and glamorous people and was accompanied by the background sounds of laughter, tinkling glasses, the soft sighs that precede lovemaking. At the other end of the spectrum, there were shouts, angry words, weeping — proof that power and position do not guarantee happiness.

And then the moment passed. The hall was once again just a lovely and impressive exhibit. I shook my head and wondered a bit at my fevered imagination. It was definitely time to leave the museum. I stepped out into the hot August afternoon and — reality.

In spite of the summer heat, I walked briskly along Avenue Georges Cinq. On the crowded avenue, I observed the urban uniform worn by tourist and native alike. It was everywhere. (Price, quality and class seemed to have little to do with it.) I saw simplistic, mundane clothing — baggy pants, shapeless jackets, tee-shirts and tired skirts, heavy peasant shoes — leveling, joyless images without pride or individuality. (And this was Paris!)

I continued to think about the exquisite clothing in the Musée and all that it represented. And I felt such a yearning for a different world — a world of extravagant style and inspiring, uplifting beauty.

How sad, I thought. And how foolish we women are. We have followed the Pied Piper designers who take their inspiration from the drones on the street or from MTV rappers and street walkers. Yes, we're really hanging out with a tough crowd these days.

And we have abandoned those cultured and loyal fashion friends who lovingly told little white lies to our public; who were supportive and encouraging; who helped us to look and feel vital, young, beautiful — or mysterious and fascinating. Whether couture thoroughbreds or their knockoff cousins, these were clothes that built us up, slimmed us down, and presented us to our public with a visual fanfare.

How much better to spend time with those charming companions than this uncompromising, cold-eyed clique of current fashionistas. They who have little knowledge of the clever dart, the unexpected bias cut, the disciplines of superb tailoring. Instead, they insist on clinical reality and create minimalist, unstructured styles that are so cruelly demanding.

I was almost at my destination, late lunch with friends at Fouquet's. As I turned the corner onto the Champs-Elysées, I thought about comtesse du Z– and the baronne de D –. And still in my nostalgic mood, I wondered. Suppose they were joining us?

What in the world would they be wearing?

2

Women
and
Their Hats

Women and Their Hats

On this Friday night at the Marina Safeway, the check-out line is long. As usual, it is composed of impatient, Today people. They fidget, scowl, or barely hide their amused smiles as they watch her, the old woman in the improbable hat. It is an elaborate, garden-party hat, worn with a once fashionable tailored pantsuit. In all, an extraordinary costume, placing her just this side of Bag Lady image.

Flowers, bees and ribbons cling to the oversized hat brim. They tremble in agitation as she struggles with her change purse, fumbling for crumpled dollars and laboriously counting out dimes, nickels, and pennies with exasperating exactness.

"The State really should do something for these people," someone mutters irritably. But as I look at the old woman (and that hat), I don't see a poor old victim at all. I see a courageous warrior, donning once again that armor which served her so well in times past. Unexpectedly, she flashes a charming and apologetic smile. Her face is suddenly radiant, and the bored checker melts. "Just take your time, lady," he says soothingly.

As I observe this little scene, I am reminded of an insightful essay by the great French writer Colette. She wrote about old ladies and the hats they choose. She noted that while, to the casual eye, an old woman wearing flamboyant, rakish or flirtatious millinery seems out of touch (even a bit batty!), in reality these hats are carefully chosen and are very significant. To Colette, they revealed the role the woman played in her youth, bringing back comforting memories.

But it seems to me that there's even more to it than that. In truth, these hats represent the unchanged essence of the woman — her statement of the Goddess within, if you will. Though society may see only a pitiable gray shadow, a woman who is now faded and fragile, her triumphs forgotten by the world, the Hat represents a tiny flame that still burns, warming the aging heart of the coquette, the gamin, or the *femme fatale*.

We might assume that this Hat Statement applies only to that generation of "hatty" women who wore hats and headgear on every possible occasion. But actually, hats and headdresses have always been tattletales, sending potent and powerful messages about the social status and the sexual and emotional climate of the wearer. Whether it be Nefertiti's obelisk headdress (the only royal wife ever to wear that sacred symbol) or Miss America in her rhinestone crown, hats and headdresses not only tell us how to value the woman underneath the hat. They tell the woman how to value herself.

At various times in the past, women's hats have been delicious concoctions — think *belle époque*, the *Moulin Rouge* and *gaité parisienne*. In this period (1890-1910), the most extreme and fantastic hats were worn, especially by the women of the *demimonde*, iron butterflies who lived for love. What incredible hats they wore! These oversized floating flower gardens bestowed grace and elegance to the delicate necks and heads that held them up. And they created for these women, who lived in a half-world of social acceptance, a powerful image of pampered indulgence. No wonder they were envied by their wifely counterparts.

At other times, women's headdress has been severe and humbling.

For example, the modest white caps of the Pilgrim women. What were they thinking, those elder statesmen of the church who formed a sort of Fashion Police to monitor all overt millinery messages? ("Let's not allow color of any kind. Who knows? It might be flattering. Unthinkable!") And so the women of the time wore nun-like headdresses, totally devoid of drama or emotion, symbolizing a way of life devoted to a patriarchal and unforgiving God. In this drab, black and white world, it's amazing that there weren't more scarlet letters!

The bonnets of the Victorians tell us everything about the lives of the women of that period. These oversized scoop-shaped hats encased a woman's face, restricting her view — much like the blinders on a horse. This was the headdress of women whose narrow lives were devoted to meekly serving husband and family. Any woman who wore her bonnet pushed back, away from her face (giving her full view of the world), was looked upon with stern disapproval by Victorian society.

But what to make of today's hats? At a time in history when women in the Western world are unarguably living a unique, free, and powerful life, most of the hats they choose for themselves are drab and deflating, the kind of hat one would see on a homeless waif in a doorway. (I'm reminded of Professor Higgins' description of guttersnipe Eliza as "…a squashed cabbage leaf".)[3] Today's hats belie the feminist message that "You *can* have it all…right now." Something is definitely wrong!

Let me give you an example of what I mean. Last night on the TV series *Once and Again*, that exquisite Sela Ward (Lilly), on her way to a significantly romantic meeting with lover Rick, pulls on a hat. Can I really call it a hat? It is a shapeless black cylinder, completely covering that glorious cloud of dark hair. (And with no forgiving lines to soften or distract from Ward's rather outsized nose.) What a curious choice.

Where is the romance, the flirtation, the femininity of a glorious hat? Today, these are almost forbidden words, to be expurgated from the politically-correct life-script of contemporary woman. (But interestingly, they are found in abundance in best-selling Romance novels.) Why reject these valuable sentiments? They can be the delectable accompaniment to our sexual encounters, creating the alchemy that transforms rough, impersonal sex to romance, love, and that loaded word…commitment.

Look and you'll see these "squashed cabbage leaves" everywhere. Julia Roberts in that movie a couple of seasons ago…gorgeous Julia in clumsy jackboots and a heavy-hearted, shapeless hat. No wonder she was a runaway bride!

And elfin Calista Flockhart, whose TV heroine Ally McBeal wore similarly defeatist hats. *Of course*, she couldn't find the fulfilling relationship she longed for. Now don't misunderstand. I'm not saying that her character's romantic failures were because her hats were unflattering! Not at all. Rather, these hats mirrored the half-realized woman who was wearing them, a woman incapable of rich, emotional fulfillment. I often wonder what amazing plot-turns might have unfolded if she once, just once, had the experience of wearing a romantic, flirtatious, *sexy* hat. (The series might never have been canceled.)

Femme fatales have always understood hats.

My all time favorite is Marlene Dietrich. Not for her a bleak, "This is me. Take it or leave it" minimalism. No. She (with designer Travis Banton) created dreams and exotic fantasies in her costumes and hats.

To my mind, the best of all is a hat she wears in *Shanghai Express*.[4] Well, no, I've never actually seen this Thirties classic. But you probably remember the scene, too. Because it is so evocative, it's excerpted in all the anthologies about Great Movies and Movie Stars.

All we need to know is that Marlene is on the Chinese frontier, traveling on the Shanghai Express and wearing a tiny, tip-tilted hat with a black lace veil. It shadows her heavy-lidded eyes and accents a gleaming, lip-rouged mouth. La Dietrich completes this costume with a black crepe dress and large *coque* feathered boa. Just the thing for train travel on the Chinese frontier! But who cares? Thirties heartthrob Clive Brook is enthralled (and so are we) as she lures him with her veiled glance.

I don't know that we can characterize Monica Lewinsky as a *femme fatale*, but she certainly had some kind of special sexual confidence, this pudgy, undistinguished 90210 girl who set her cap for a President. And what a cap! Berets have always been street-girl tarty — never mind the DKNY label. This French peasant's cap was popularized by that eternal *gamin* Chanel, and it has always sent an "I'm a good-time girl" message.

Compare Monica's soft-to-the-touch velvety beret to Hillary's hats.

So much has been written about the Clinton relationship, but the hats tell it all. Bad Boy Bill. Responsible Hillary. And a Girl in a Beret.

Hillary often wears large, peach-basket hats. An alternative to waif caps, these are favored by today's Strong Women. These hats send their millinery message very clearly. Weighty. Powerful. No-nonsense. These are hats that sail into meetings and conferences and *take charge*.

But then, leaders have perennially known how to throw their weight around through voluminous garments and headdresses, sartorial splendor that made them larger than life. It's elemental and territorial. The inflated size of these peach-basket hats simply take up more space. Their large, inflexible brims keep people at a respectful distance. There's no doubt about it, these are hats that can be "thrown into the ring!"

In no way are today's oversized power-hats to be confused with the large brimmed hats of more romantic times.

I'm thinking of the barbecue scene in *Gone With The Wind*,[5] for example. Scarlett, the quintessential Southern Belle, wears an oversized beribboned straw hat. Its soft, pliable brim creates sensuous dips and curving lines around that kitten face, accenting every flirtatious smile and sideways glance. Rhett Butler appears. (It's the first time we've seen him, but we're in love already.) His hat is eloquent, too. A dashing white Panama with an important brim... a rogue's hat that promises masculine strength and sexual power. And what do today's men wear on their heads? Boy's caps. Baseball caps. Worn backwards! Is it any wonder the battle of the sexes rages?

Perhaps Hillary Clinton caught some of this hat hierarchism from the British Royals. Certainly, the two most influential first ladies of the twentieth century made regal hat statements — Hillary's large queenly hats and Princess Jackie's signature off-the-face pillbox.

You may have noticed that the British royal ladies *always* wear hats. What to make of this impossible headgear? Great saucers or bowls, veritable salads of veils, flowers, and puffed up tulle, plopped upon their regal heads. More than anything else, these hats seem determinedly unflattering to those long, sad, Windsor faces.

But of course, these are not hats at all. Rather, they are symbolic crowns. Crowns do not have to be jeweled to carry their weighty message of privilege, power, and authority. And he (or she) who wears a crown doesn't care a fig if it's flattering or not. One had better not look askance at any of these royal toppers, or it could be "off with your head!"

The power of hats has not been lost on those who comment upon and chronicle America's royalty. It started with Hedda Hopper, whose extravagant hats helped to give her the *gravitas* to be the outspoken arbiter of manners and morals in the Golden Age of Hollywood. And San Francisco's premiere movie critic Jan Wahl carries on this tradition. She, too, always wears an impressive Power Hat.

Movie costume has always provided us with an eloquent psycho-cultural shorthand. So, we can trace the changing psyche of women through their movie millinery. In the Twenties, the dizzy excitement and sexual freedom of pre-Depression days was represented by deep *cloches* (literally "bell" in French) that accented the hot, smoldering eyes of Pola Negra and Gloria Swanson, the jazz-baby orbs of Joan Crawford. What a rude awakening the "crash" brought to that carefree world! (They didn't call it The Depression for nothing.) And the movie moguls wisely gave sad and shaken audiences what they craved...escape.

Movie studios in the Thirties and early Forties produced a string of screwball comedies. (The first, according to movie historians, was Capra's *It Happened One Night*.)[6] These were movies about hare-brained heiresses, daffy debutantes, spunky girl reporters.

And these madcap heroines wore hats that were all that the name implies... saucy, perky, zany hats that perched on the heads of stars like Carole Lombard (gorgeous and funny, a rare combination), Irene Dunne (*Theodora Goes Wild*), Paulette Goddard (the ever capricious child-wife), and even the inscrutable Garbo (in *Ninotchka*).[7]

Legendary film designer Adrian created many of these hats which seem to be forerunners of Flying Saucers. They perched on the side of the head or tipped over one eye, appearing ready to *zoom* off at the next plot twist. Often, they were pierced with a single dramatic feather. These hats were the defining statement for a world of carefree and silly escapades…a world so far from the stark realities of the Thirties.

This tells us about movie millinery. But what does it say about the women of that era? Perhaps it tells us that you could find courage in a hat. If you had to pound the pavement in a desperate job search, wearing a tired and threadbare dress, slipping cardboard into down-at-heel pumps… well, the lift of a lighthearted hat was a treasure. You could also "get-by" with one good black crepe dress and a classic pair of shoes for season after season. All you needed to buy was a wonderful hat.

The hats of World War II movies tell a dual story, no doubt reflecting the ambivalence of women who were now forced to play two roles. For husbands and lovers, they were the focus of poignant memories and postponed desire, enshrined in wallet portraits and barrack wall galleries. While at home, in their real world, women were moving into new, uncharted waters, reluctantly taking on all the responsibilities of home, family, and jobs in airplane and munitions factories.

The idealized image of women became super-feminine. (This was, after all, the era of the thrusting, structured bra.)

Wartime restrictions on fabrics and manpower, however, meant that elaborate fashions had to sit on the sidelines for the duration. Clothes (and movie costumes) were simple and narrow, thereby using less fabric. Tailored suits with padded, "Joan Crawford shoulders" helped women to carry their new responsibilities. Simple, formfitting crepe dresses, sensuously draped, expressed the goddess image.

But when it came to the hats... well, you could lose your head! Movie millinery of the time became quite fantastic. For example, in *Cover Girl*,[8] screen goddess Rita Hayworth wears a large organza picture hat with matching gloves (very *chic* in the Forties), also a flowered turban, and several other extravagant designs. These hats, combined with her long, glamour girl red hair would make these styles seem over the top today.

But in the Fantastic Forties, there was no such thing. And when "he" came home on furlough, real life women were also creating fantasies in their choice of glamourous hats and dresses, treasured visions for him to take back to the war-zone.

When wartime women were playing their other role, the hats were no-nonsense. Neither sexy nor flirtatious, we see a feminized version of a man's hat, though not quite the hat of today's free feminist. No, these women were being thrust into a new and challenging world. And so we see that the typical hat was like a large, *softened* man's hat (a fedora, if you will), with a large brim often worn flipped up in the back, snapped down in the front. These are Responsible Hats. In capital letters.

No scene from the movies expresses the Responsible Forties Woman better than that famous last scene in *Casablanca*. You know the one. The Nazis are fast approaching the tiny airfield, brakes screeching at every high speed turn in the road. Sinister Conrad Veidt, furiously honking the horn, pushes his sleek Deusenburg to ever faster speeds. And the clock is ticking. The small plane, motors revving, is ready to take off.

Standing close together in the swirling fog (Fog? This is North Africa! Oh well…) Ingrid and Rick ("Bogie," of course) are saying their good-byes. Or is it really good-bye? Will she, at the last moment, throw it all aside for passion? Leave her husband? Run off across the tarmac with the love-of-her-life? Of course not! No need for Rick to go into his noble little speech about "… the problems of three little people (that) don't amount to a hill of beans in this crazy world…"[9]

We already *know* Ingrid's decision. She's wearing a Responsible Hat. Now, if she were wearing a beret or a skittish little cap with a feather. Or even if she had pulled off that hat, tossed her hair… Ah, that would have been another story.

While the Responsible Hat of the Forties represented a pseudo-man's hat, a sort of bisexual millinery, a woman wearing an authentic man's hat creates a powerfully erotic image. It's very clear. There is something terribly sexy and appealing about a woman wearing an actual item of men's clothing. (Wearing men's pajamas is pretty sexy, too.)

Here again, the movies give us such graphic examples. You know about Dietrich, of course. She made movie history in her very first appearance on an American screen wearing a man's top-hat. And a tuxedo, too. But let's move to the Forties and that movie siren Rita Hayworth. I do hope you've rented the video of *Blood and Sand*,[10] if only to see Hayworth in hot pink gown and gaucho hat, a fabulously alluring image, copied recently by Catherine Zeta-Jones in *Mask of Zorro*.[11]

The hats of the Fifties can be described in two little words: Doris Day. Doris, in sweet little Good Wife hats, epitomized a postwar ideal for women that make the Stepford Wives look like a group of wild and swinging Party Girls. Home. Family. Hubby. In the Fifties, that was *it*.

The social revolution that we call the Sixties did indeed start in the early Sixties, but continued on into the Seventies. And women's hats continued to tell their revealing stories of woman's inner life.

Typical of times that are maelstroms of cultural upheaval, the girl-woman becomes the ideal. (Take a quick glance back to the Twenties, or even a longer view back to the French Revolution. See what I mean?) Remember, this was the era of waif-like Twiggy and super model (the "Shrimp") Jean Shrimpton. The hats they (and we) wore were doll-hats: close fitting, Courreges-inspired toy helmets (reminiscent of the Twenties *cloche*). Or large, off-the-face, school girl boaters. Breezy, toss-in-the-air, light hearted hats.

But as the revolution continued, the social climate changed. Rebellious little girls grew up and threw off that final symbol of male domination — The Hat.

If Sixties movies gave us hats (those *divine* Givenchy hats in *Breakfast at Tiffany's*)[12], well, women knew it was all a dream. In the real world, no one wore hats. Not even to weddings. Weddings? "Baby, Don't Get Hooked on Me."[13] "By the Time I Get to Phoenix"[14]... you'll know it was just about good sex, good times, and goodbye. So women became tough, wary, and sexually cynical. Instead of hats, many women wore gypsy-style scarves, creating for themselves a shrewd, crafty image that said: "I've Got a New Attitude."[15]

So here we are, in the beginning of a new millennium, and these "nothing" hats that so many women wear today seem to me to speak of a sort of emotional exhaustion. After this bumpy, forty year ride, women are asking, "Who am I?"

Believe it or not, a significant hat can help you find out. Even if a woman isn't suffering from an emotional identity crisis, the right hat can open up whole new vistas in her emotional landscape. And can reveal the many facets of the Goddess within.

For example, those Homburg/Derby hats worn by the girls in the band in *Cabaret*.[16] This is the hat that really speaks to the slut in all of us. What dark, shadowy, sexual images these hats evoke! Strictly forget-flowers-and-dinner, get-to-the-bottom-line sort of sexual messages. (Next Halloween, do you dare?)

Speaking of sex — steamy and otherwise — let's talk about the birds, the bees, and the flowers for a minute. There's a sound reason why the most successful hats often include these elements. Tendrils and vines, in the form of ribbons, also play a part. If I have inspired you to shop for A Hat — and yes, they are out there — keep in mind what I am about to tell you.

When your parents told you about the birds and the bees those many years ago, I have no doubt they left out this very essential but little known fact. Men are very much like birds and bees. They are *attracted* by the same things — flowers, fragrance, and bright colors. I shall leave the discussion of fragrance to another time, but let's see how hats — or the right hat — can create for a woman a magnetism and beauty that will surprise and delight her.

The next time you are invited to an elegant wedding, dare to wear a wonderful hat. A hat that is a *melange* of meltingly romantic colors. Or *red*.

Perhaps a hat with a swooning brim. Or a tiny hat composed of nothing so much as an oversized pink rose, dipping over one eye, creating for each glance a world of implications. Or perhaps you'll do a Dietrich, and choose something with a mysterious, eye-shadowing veil.

You think you know everything? Try it. You'll see. Hats have magic powers. They not only tell audiences wonderful things about (newly) wonderful you. A fabulous hat can tell you important, mysterious, empowering things about yourself.

Proust must have been talking about the effect of a magnificent hat when he described "...the wild and supernal joy that sweeps over you when you know yourself to be beautiful."[17]

3

Entrenched

Entrenched

*T*he Couture runways of every fashion season — since the Thirties, anyway — have seen at least one version of the perennial Trench Coat. Like the most popular girl at the senior prom, The Trench is asked to dance every dance, whether it's slinking down the ramp at Valentino, flirting along Chanel's *rue de la mode*, or nodding hello to the front row disciples at Karan or Lauren.

This favorite garment seems to live a charmed fashion life, appearing flawlessly *chic* year after year. It's always Just Right, whether shown in the classic gabardine or unexpectedly in lamé, mink, tweed, or organza. (In fact, I have just purchased a Parisian *prêt à porté* version in blue denim — short, sassy, irresistible!)

If we take The Trench at face value, we find it easy to understand its ongoing popularity and appeal. Like a face with good bones and all the right proportions, The Trench is immediately pleasing. It combines functionality (a woman's garment with *pockets*) and a certain masculine brio.

No doubt about it, when a woman puts on a Trench Coat, she feels the same way one feels in certain cities —

New York, Paris, Vienna. There is the distinct possibility that something wonderful, dramatic, and unexpected is about to happen.

For example, suppose you're in Manhattan hurrying along East 76th on a very gray, cold day, the collar of your Trench snapped up, the belt (unbuckled, of course) is pulled tightly and knotted. It doesn't seem too far-fetched to imagine a tall and handsome stranger charging out of The Carlyle, striding along beside you for a few paces, then suddenly sweeping you into a close embrace. He whispers, "Quick, pretend you're with me...."

Yes, the Trench Coat carries with it a glamour and presence, like a person with a fascinating inner life, sensed rather than spoken. In movie lingo, The Trench has a powerful "back story." Are you familiar with the term? It's a device used by both screenwriters and actors. It simply means creating for each character a history, a background, a series of specific details which may have no bearing on the present events in the story. However, this backstory history is essential to the fleshing out of the character, and can mean the difference between a critic's ho-hum and an Academy Award.

Did that character who is seen in the movie to be poor, discouraged and heading for disaster originally come from an influential family and a life of privilege and pleasure? Then how much more meaningful that failure becomes when we, the audience, are told of this backstory with some tiny clue. In his garret studio (through the camera's probing eye), we spot an ornate crystal inkwell on the battered desk. Or an unexpectedly luxurious lining to a threadbare coat is glimpsed, for just a moment, as the character huddles in a snow-banked doorway.

In another movie (*Waterloo Bridge*,[18] for example), the heroine may be seen as the toast of society, but perhaps her past is murky indeed, making her triumphs that much sweeter. And the gifted actress will be able to play on this back story. She will portray, in the midst of her character's social victories, a shadow of fear behind her eyes. Will someone, somehow, recognize her and remember their sordid encounter in that hidden past? Powerful stuff!

So, as I was saying, the Trench Coat has an intriguing back story. The next time you see a Trench in the glossy pages of *Vogue* or *Bazaar*, blink once, twice, three times…and perhaps (just like in the movies) you'll see in flashback the *real* Trench Coat.

Trench Coat. Trench! Get it? Probably not. I certainly didn't until I did some research. After all, what does "in the trenches" mean today? Slogging along on some corporate project. But in 1914, that little word carried a world of meaning — pain, panic, patriotism. Valor and victory.

Our story starts in London at 18-22, the Haymarket. Let's step out of the rain and through the doors of Burberrys, the London headquarters of the original Trench Coat. And we must establish, right off the cricket bat, that when you say Trench Coat, you really mean Burberrys.

Other offspring — de la Renta, Calvin Klein, Armani, *et al* — stem from this aristocratic British beginning.

On an ornately carved table we find a tasteful brochure. It tells us that prior to World War I, the venerable weatherproof coats produced by this company were universally known as Burberrys. And the firm proudly advertised that theirs was a coat "named by a king." Mr. Burberry had christened his invention — that is, the unique waterproof material that all Burberrys were made of — "gabardine." And early company ads refer to "T. Burberrys Gabardine." However, when King Edward IV called for his waterproof hunting coat, he'd invariably say, "Get me my Burberry!" And the name stuck.

Burberrys went along on aristocratic hunting parties at country manor houses, aboard royal yachts, and to fishing lodges in Scotland. "I have tried every conceivable garment in the shape of Macintosh...it is the first time in sixteen years that I have ever returned perfectly dry after a day's shooting in a good, old fashioned Devonshire rain...", writes the honorable Mr. V.W. in 1910.[19]

Burberry Waterproofs would keep a chap dry during the most challenging sailing adventure. And if you were "kitting up" for an elephant or tiger hunt, Burberrys ads tell you to choose their unique gabardine sporting gear "...for India and the colonies... resists hot and cold wind, rain, or thorns..." Burberrys even went along, in 1912, to the South Pole with Amunsen and "…proved (to be) good friends, indeed."[20]

But the dashing, daredevil, sporting Burberry was in for an image change. And a name change, too. A preview of this new identity could be seen at the turn of the century, when officers and generals in the Boer War chose to wear their Burberrys on that South African campaign. However, it wasn't until the Great War (as WWI was known in England) that the Trench Coat emerged.

As Burberrys official history tells us, "The Great War in 1914 introduced Trench warfare and, as ever, the Burberry adapted itself to circumstances. Epaulettes and 'D' rings for attaching equipment were added to the standard all-weather coat, which became so popular that it soon became known as 'the Trench Coat.' Between 1914 and 1918, it is established that a million Burberrys were worn by combatant officers."[21]

And no wonder. Trench warfare was brutal. It meant that, in addition to the threat of bullets and shells, one's constitution was assaulted by life in a wet and muddy trench. Soldiers might live for weeks or months in damp, cold, grave-like conditions.

The Burberry Trench Coat was the perfect garment for this bleak world, one small element that made sense in an otherwise crazy universe. And the cut and style — that inimitable style of The Trench — would give officers the costume needed to play their role. "Buck up, lads! We'll make it through all this…"

I came to realize the extreme youth of many of these original Trench Coat warriors during a long ago backpacking trip through England's hill country. On this ambitious trek, we walked miles through a verdant countryside that was dotted with picturesque villages. We skirted the grounds of impressive country manors and visited numerous country churches. The graveyards of these churches, with their old-fashioned statued gravestones, told a poignant story of the Great War. We saw countless markers remembering beloved sons who had been cut down at ages nineteen, twenty or twenty one. One in particular was deeply moving.

The size and elaborate design of the gravestone marked this as the resting place of someone of social importance. The weeping marble angel, garlanded by a climbing rose, was an eloquent messenger of grief and loss. Chiseled in the gray marble at the base of the monument were these words:

Here lies Arthur Colin Milbank
The only son of Lord and Lady Devereaux Milbank
"A noble warrior, he died valiantly leading his troops"
The Battle of Ypres, Flanders
April, 1896 - September, 1917.

Arthur Milbank[22] would have been twenty one.

Standing there at the graveside on that misty afternoon, I felt a wave of compassion for the tragedy embodied in those few lines. Three words seemed to stand out from the rest — "The only son…."

What was he like, I wondered? One could imagine Arthur's parents, perhaps rather older than is usual, and their delight in producing, at last, such a magnificent son and heir. I think he would have been tall. Slender, yet strong, with fair hair and steady blue eyes. And Arthur (I continued to imagine) had been like his namesake, a noble knight. He had been a shining example of *noblesse oblige*, that is, the obligation of the nobility to justify their privileged status by being exquisitely courteous, mindful of social responsibilities, and brave in protecting the weak and defenseless.

At school, one could see that Arthur had been the natural leader of his school mates and the worshipped hero of knobby-knee'd First-Form boys. So, of course, as soon as he was able, Arthur did the Right Thing. He joined the regiment, and went off on his noble cause, to win the War To End All Wars.

There would have been a girl, too, mad about him in her patrician way. She knew, somehow, even before the telegram came. Arthur would not be coming back.

> *The poppies in Belgium are not like our California poppies, slim and tailored and golden. No, the poppies on Flanders fields have soft, open petals, creating cups*

of brilliant crimson. On this September afternoon. after an onslaught of rain, the cheerful blossoms droop disconsolately on delicate stems.

They seem to grow more profusely in this small hollow at the base of a rock-laden, sloping field. And there, amongst mud-spattered poppies, lies the body of Arthur Colin Milbank. Fair hair tousled and darkly matted on his left temple, his china-blue eyes are still wide open in surprise. The rest of his face is mercifully shielded from our gaze by the turned-up collar of his Trench Coat.

The Trench Coat served as a shroud for Arthur and for so many others. But for those who did come back, the coat became a staple of everyday wear in damp and soggy England. And perhaps, recognizing what the Trench Coat had been through and all that it represented, it became a sort of White Knight's armor and a badge of urban courage.

Contemporary warriors got the message. The coat would become the perfect uniform for Bogart's on-screen *persona*; an ordinary guy, reluctantly doing what he has to do, greatness thrust upon him. Columbo's character is cut from the same cloth — doing his unpleasant job, relentlessly seeking out evildoers — another noble, unwilling hero.

It's easy to see why women have embraced The Trench. We can use its implications of strength, courage, power.

Hang-Ups, The Secret Life of Clothes

Power? Yes. Because Beauty *is* Power. And as every designer knows, the Trench can be a spectacularly glamourous garment on almost every woman.

When did the Trench Coat first appear in women's wardrobes? We can be specific about its debut on the fashion scene. Flashback to the Thirties and we see the ubiquitous Trench again making a dramatic move, this time into the movies and then, into the wardrobes of fashionable women everywhere.

And what an all-star cast for the film debut of this sartorial classic — Greta Garbo and legendary film designer Adrian. In the movie *Anna Christie*,[23] Adrian designed a Trench Coat for the glorious star. It looked so sensational that women clamored for look-alike versions. (What a bonanza for those knockoff artists on Seventh Avenue!) In fact, the success of this one design inspired Adrian to launch his own couture career a few years later.

We see the nonstop allure of the Trench Coat in so many memorable movie scenes, wrapped around so many gorgeous stars — beauty redefined for each generation: Katherine Hepburn in her glamourous prime; lynx-eyed Lauren Bacall; the eternal Marlene. And Audrey Hepburn — in *Breakfast at Tiffany's*,[24] she created for the Trench Coat yet another indelible cinematic image. Audrey, standing in the rain, laughing through her tears, her alley cat protected from the downpour, tucked inside the front of her beige Trench.

One of my favorite Trench Coat scenes occurs in that *film noir* classic *Laura*.[25] The star Gene Tierney wears a *white* Trench (designer Bonnie Cashin's version of the classic coat) in a pivotal scene. Do you know the movie? In this scene, the hero-detective (and we, the audience) believe that Laura Hunt has been murdered. In flashback, we learn of her triumphs in the upper echelons of New York's corporate and society worlds. She was beautiful, bright, successful. And incredibly alluring. Quite a package!

The camera follows the detective (Dana Andrews) as he prowls Laura's upper East Side apartment, investigating the site of her murder. He moves from room to elegant room, each one so evocative of her presence. He reads her love letters, checks out the clothes in her closet. He samples her scent in the crystal perfume bottles on a mirrored dressing table. With each detail, he becomes more infatuated with this beautiful woman. Entranced, he moves into the living room, mixes a drink, switches on the record player to hear the record that had been left there. ("…what was her mood, that last night of her life?")

The haunting melody from the spinning platter fills the room. He settles into a deep chair. By now half in love with the enigmatic victim, he contemplates her life-sized portrait, hanging above the mantel. He nods, then falls asleep, still caught in the dream of her loveliness. So are we. She was so young. So beautiful. We feel cheated that this marvelous heroine is dead, viewed by us only in movie flashback.

But wait! While Mark (the detective) sleeps, we hear the sound of a key in the lock. Slowly, slowly…the door opens. And there is Laura. She's alive, exquisite as we knew she would be, wearing a marvelous hat and that sensational *white* Trench Coat. Zowie! Whatta scene.

What happens next? It's rentable. Crank up the VCR. (You'll *love* it.)

And what of the latest chapter in the history of The Trench? While the Trench Coat itself has become a time-less design, an icon of dégagé style, the parent company Burberry has remained conservative. And a bit dull. You might characterize it as the "Queen Mother" amongst venerable fashion houses.

Asked to describe a Burberry "Mac," a shopper on London's fashionable Beauchamp Place said, "The Burberry? It's kind of what your 'Mum' wore…" Well, what can you expect of a brand that's been around for a hundred years?

Apparently, shareholders have expected a lot more. And in 2001, they passed that message along to the new CEO of Burberrys — American fashion powerhouse Rosemarie Bravo. The new designer is Roberto Menighetti. This daring team has ushered in another metamorphosis for our hero. (And it turns out to be an undercover story.) Enter… the Hip Trench.

You remember that the Burberry Trench Coat has traditionally had a signature check lining. On its one hundredth year anniversary (1901-2001), the stalwart pattern that, undercover, had accompanied various explorers, Boer war generals, and brave officers on Flanders fields and beyond, that distinctive crimson, black and camel plaid turned the classic image inside out.

In 2001, that vibrant plaid came jiggling down the runways of London, Paris, and New York. The signature check appeared in trendy coats, miniskirts, bustiers, 'gators, nifty caps, faddish bags. (Would you believe a Burberry plaid mink clutch @ $1,750?) There was even a Trench "coat" for your favorite Yorky, Poodle, or *canine du jour*. ($235 – assorted sizes.) And for the truly hip (aka Whitney Houston and Celine Dion), the house check was made-up in sleek stretch fabric and MTV styles…" the better to see you, my dear."

Ah, well, times change. As Anatole France observed, if you would know a society or civilization, do not look to their history books but to their fashions. And *yup*, it's all there. In a world that sometimes seems turned upside down and inside out, New York designer Miguel Anrover showed a Trench dress in the signature Burberry check. It had been created by turning a vintage Trench Coat inside out and back to front!

And would they have cared, those early devotees of the Burberry Trench Coat? Would they chafe at this transmogrification and bemoan the loss of those basic British values of understatement and tradition? Are you kidding? As I've said, many of those World War I trench warriors were very young. (In fact, statistically, the great majority of men who died in that war were under thirty!)

I think these young bucks would relish the sight of shapely thighs, a perky "bum" and generous "knockers" encased in Burberry plaid. They would revel in the lusty desire that these images would inspire. Young or mature, they would delight in this parade of youth and beauty. And the subliminal message that Life Goes On.

4
High
Heels

High Heels

*M*ost of the women I know have a collection of high heels.

Are you a collector, too?

Then you know that we shoe collectors live with closets that, whatever their size, are cluttered and stacked with boxes of high-heels; pumps, sandals, slides, platforms. In classic leather, snakeskin, patent leather, suede, and gilded kidskin. Or unlikely materials such as plastic, *faux* zebra (yes, we all know that was a mistake…), denim, poppy printed crepe, etc., etc.

The shape and size of the heels themselves is a motley mix — thick, thin, slender, rounded. They are as varied as the thighs at a Miss Universe contest.

Somehow, these shoes never seem to be thrown away or recycled. They lounge in the closet, *odalisques* waiting for their moments of fulfillment. For those past their prime, such moments never come. Still, we can't part with them. So we sacrifice orderly closets to provide shelter and security for these former companions, in recognition of past services and potent memories.

Just what is there about high heels? Plenty! They're pleasure and pain, erotic and wonderful, symbols of sexual awareness and proclivities, a rite of passage, and a never-fail witch's spell. They also seem to be part of a woman's DNA.

How else to explain the shrieks of glee when I gifted a friend's three-year-old with a collection of tiny-girl-sized, high heeled, lucite slides. "It's all she wanted for her birthday — and she sleeps with them," her perplexed mother (who wears neither lucite nor high heeled slides) told me.

But little girls grow up and move far beyond the innocent fantasies of dress-up. And then, high heels take on deeper meaning and significance. While psychiatrists and sociologists have yet to explore my DNA theory, they have had much to say about women's shoes, and high heels in particular. That old rascal Freud explained, in multitudinous notes, that shoes are very erotic indeed.

And if you don't believe *him*, Bette Midler said it, too: "The woman who understands shoes, understands *everything!*" I mean, it's no coincidence that the pivotal element in the world's most famous love story was a shoe — and you can bet that Cinderella's glass slipper wasn't a frumpy Flat.

Shoes, whether high-heeled or not, tell us much about the wearer. "Put your best foot forward" is powerful advice, acknowledging, albeit unconsciously, the visual impact of shoes. "Well-heeled," "Down at heel" and even "Round heels" are three different takes on the powerful symbolism of shoes — and heels in particular.

Okay, so what are shoes telling us? Men's and women's shoes say different things. A man's shoes are (hopefully) like the man himself. Sturdy, substantial, strong. He can stand on his own two feet. Heavy workman's shoes imply a rustic virility... the "natural man" challenging the elements. Today's ubiquitous running shoes typecast the ever-youthful, nonconformist athlete. Elegant, finely-made shoes tell another, more sophisticated story. A bit more androgynous, they bespeak wealth (a really good pair of men's dress shoes are pricey indeed) and power, two fabled aphrodisiacs. The Gucci-type, tasseled loafer adds another element to this picture...power, wealth, and the leisure to enjoy it.

As you might expect, women's shoes send more elaborate and varied messages. After all, we're much more complicated creatures than the stalwart male. And our shoes show it.

Contemporary woman can run the gamut — shoewise — from lucite slides to the most masculine styles imaginable. Today, women as well as men may be wearing heavy brogues, behemoth biker boots, pneumatic running shoes. However, as of this writing, delicate, high-heeled shoes are the sole prerogative of women. (But stay tuned!)

The allure of Woman is both infinite and ever-changing, as we see if we take a backward look at the shoe fashions of the last forty years. There's the Natural Woman, found wearing the sandals of the Sixties; the Dress-for-Success pump, worn by the upwardly mobile striver of the Eighties; the "Just Do It" Nike heroine of the Nineties projecting a sex-is-healthy-sport kind of image.

And what is the shoe of the new millennium? Well, it's high heels — hands-down! Why? There are a couple of reasons. First, they are the final, drop-the-other shoe iconoclastic statement in the feminist manifesto. We've proven that we *can* have it all (if we want it). And that includes make-up, flirty short skirts, and high-heels.

Also, as clothes themselves have retreated as an important fashion element, shoes become paramount. I mean, what do you really *need* today beyond some great jeans, a couple of skirts, two dozen Gap T-shirts and a color-coordinated cellphone? You need high-heels!

And the latest issues of *Vogue, Bazaar,* "W", *et al,* tout that need, and regularly devote pages reporting in depth the latest shoe fashions and the designer stars who create them. At the top of the list is Manolo Blahnik, darling of super models (Niki Taylor), movie stars (Julia Roberts, Jennifer Lopez), MTV Divas (Madonna), royalty (princesses from Monaco to Denmark), and the breathless fashion press. A recent profile in *Vogue* explained that, "Elegant women crave his shoes because of their 'erotic charge.' He's taken shoes out of the accessories ghetto and given them their independence."[26]

Other kindred "soles" are Parisian shoe designer Bruno Frisoni and Italian master cobbler Rene Caovilla. Frisoni believes that "…dynamite shoes can alter a woman's entire outlook". Caovilla's designs attract some of the world's premier design houses, *i.e.* Valentino, Dior. They come to his factory near Venice where their most extravagant and capricious runway fantasies become reality.

It's clear that, orthopedic arguments to the contrary, high heels are here to stay. The sociological implications and emotional appeal of high heels is so powerful, I'm afraid that the Dr. Scholl's of this world are shouting into the wind when they condemn the style.

Podiatrists aren't the only experts who look askance at high heels. Male anthropologists and sociologists, when discussing women's high heels, conclude (with irritating chauvinism) that "…the appeal of the high heeled shoe is that the female's body is posed provocatively, the pelvis thrust forward seductively, thus telegraphing a message of sexual availability to the male…" Availability, indeed! What do they know?

I say that high heels mean one thing. High heels are Power — as any cowboy, Houston oil man, or Vegas showgirl will tell you. In fact, high heels (so the story goes) were invented by a *man* to add to his stature and power. One of the French Louis (the XIVth to be precise) had a pair of high heels designed for the royal tootsies. And the rest is history!

Killer heels can contribute much to a woman's history, too. When a woman slips on a pair of high heels, look out! With this one clothing choice, she immediately doubles her power — her sexual power. You can test it yourself. The next time you're on your way out to the local Starbuck's on a Saturday morning, wearing your casual Saturday morning face, hair, jeans and T-shirt, slide into a pair of 4" heels rather than your usual running shoes. Just see how fast you get waited-on. (You'll get extra *latte*, too. It always works.)

Let's remember that high heels are inherently phallic symbols. So, when a woman slips on a pair of high heels, she not only *possesses* a penis (thereby fulfilling that universal yearning, if we can believe Freud), she is also able to dominate that penis with every deliciously defiant step. And there's something about this rather kinky combination that seems to drive men wild. (Go figure.)

The impact of high heels is not to be confused with other types of elevated shoes. For example, the towering cleated shoes of Japanese classic costume, whose purpose is to hobble the woman and prevent her from running away. This is a familiar theme in the history of women's fashions, even though it is a theme usually "clothed" in various aesthetic, pseudo-religious, or erotic explanations.

Shall we go down this intriguing path for just a moment? I can give you several other examples.

If we look at the fashions of the Western world, we see that at times, clothes have nearly immobilized women. Think hoop skirts, corsets, layers of lace and crinoline.

And then there's the fashion that came right out and said it: hobble skirts. This was a style (circa 1914) which was wrapped so closely around the knees and calves that walking became almost impossible. A woman was reduced to a geisha-girl type of eager little trot. In a filmed interview, a very aged Chanel described these hobble skirts, fashionable in her youth. She explained that a woman couldn't even step off a curb without leaning on the steadying arm of her male escort.

Think of it. In effect, a woman could never go out without an escort, companion (or keeper!). These skirts, Chanel explained, were one of the inspirations for her entire fashion philosophy. Et voila! Enter the short, pleated, swingy skirts, loose-fitting shirtwaists and jackets, and easy two-toned pumps of the Chanel legend. Freedom![27]

A much more sinister aspect of costume is the actual deformity of Woman's body to accomplish this goal of enforced helplessness (all in the name of that perennial fall-guy, Fashion). I'm thinking, of course, of the Chinese custom of binding a woman's feet. This process would be started at an early age and would continue until maturity. The ideal result was a tiny foot, arched in much the same way as a ballet dancer's foot en pointe. In a recent TV travel documentary, a very old Chinese woman revealed that women of the time were very proud of their tiny feet, and willingly endured the pain and ensuing physical limitation.

A bit on the lighter side is a custom from ancient Ethiopia where the royal princesses were positively noodled to make them enormously fat and thereby totally immobilized. Apparently, the custom also made them irresistible. (If you have just, for the umpteenth time, denied yourself a calorie-loaded chocolate treat, you may join me in thinking, "Ahhh, to be in old Ethiopia!")

But let's continue with our examination of high heels. Worn judiciously, they neither deform nor hobble. And they project an undeniable youthfulness and vitality. Did you notice that the Queen Mother of England, on her 100th birthday, was still valiantly wearing little high heeled pumps?

High heels also create for women a connection with exciting male archetypes, all of whom wear a version of a high-heeled boot: gypsy kings in their elaborately decorated fine leather boots; smoldering Argentine gauchos and super-stud cowboys; Flamenco dancers; and Texas movers and shakers in their Tony Lima's. Powerful stuff! And a woman in high-heeled boots takes on some of this exotic mystique.

When a woman is not wearing high heels, what's the message that low-heels are projecting? A pair of Nikes or similar running shoes imply the power of health, strength, and stamina. Ankle boots, worn with pants or jeans, create a tough, "kick-ass" image. Low heeled, practical, no-nonsense shoes are the uniform of the Good Girls of this world — dutiful, steady, compliant. In movies, the faithful secretary (who may be secretly in love with her boss) always wears Sensible Shoes. By contrast, feisty heroines — *a la Erin Brockovich* — sport peep-toed killer spikes.

Let's not forget, the more uncovered the shoe, the more it projects a come-over-here-and-sit-by-me message. (This makes the high-heeled sandal a very sexy shoe indeed.) But the most seductive shoe of all is the high-heeled slide. This is the ultimate "babe" shoe, and creates an intriguing image. It suggests the potential of imminent nudity as it casually slips and slides on the arched foot. We could say it is a style that has "The Look of Love."[28] (Is your love life ailing? Heel thyself!)

In spite of their psychological impact, shoes have not always played a major role in women's fashions. Rather, they have made revealing comments about a woman's social status and sexual role. Before the Industrial Revolution, shoes made a definitive statement about social position for both men and women.

This is still true today, though in much more subtle, even esoteric terms. But in the 17th, 18th, and early 19th centuries, the message was clear: heavy shoes — crude, cobbled together brogues, clogs, wooden sabots — were a uniform of the peasants. These were foot coverings able to walk miles over muddy country roads, tend flocks, plant crops, trudge into market towns, and withstand the challenges of filthy streets.

By contrast, the aristocracy wore exquisitely crafted shoes and boots: foot coverings with pliant leather soles, delicate heels, luxurious trim. These were perfectly functional designs for a class who seldom walked, but rode in carriages or were carried in sedan chairs. Their delicate shoes (if one *must* place one's foot on the ground) were always protected by a carpet — red being the preferred color.

Skilled shoemakers crafted these shoes, slippers (as delicate shoes were called) and boots. Some of these shoes can still be seen in the museums of New York, London and Paris. To see these elegant foot-fashions is to marvel at their superb craftsmanship and intricate design.

When these shoes were asked to dance, the two shoe types — heavy and clumsy vs. delicate and light — underscored the social chasm between the commoners and the aristos.

Peasant dances are traditionally heavy-footed, with clogging and stamping types of movements. Or they are wildly athletic. However, in spite of athletic skill and verve, the movements and mood are restricted by the shoes. The dances of the nobility, by contrast, have featured pointed toes (an impossibility in heavy, peasant shoes) as well as gliding, sliding, graceful movements.

Any upstart social climber would need many sessions with an early Arthur Murray (not to mention a trip to Ferragamo's salon) to dance across that gigantic social divide. Here we see how costume can have such a defining impact on people's lives. The crude and heavy shoes of the peasants hobbled and limited them, enabling the aristocrats to characterize the peasants as inherently clumsy, awkward and uncouth.

While shoes were making these sociological statements, they were not a pivotal fashion force. In the early nineteenth century, the occasional glimpse of a foot and shoe were permitted. But Queen Victoria changed all that. In the uptight era that bears her name, shoes were not only out of the fashion spotlight, they were completely out of sight. Invisible. The strict dress codes of the time dictated that a woman's feet would not be seen at all. At least not in public.

As a result, there was a very real distinction between indoor and outdoor footwear. In her boudoir, a woman might wear a seductive little velvet slipper, but out in public, it was a modest high-buttoned or lace-up style. The point is, in Victorian times, one's public self was very prim and proper. But in the boudoir, who knows what sort of non-Victorian antics were going on?

Frankly, it's probably best not to ask, because this was undeniably an era of intense (and weird!) eroticism. And the Victorian dress code *vis-à-vis* a woman's shoes, gave implicit recognition that the glimpse of a woman's foot, clad in a shapely, delicate, colorful shoe (peeping out from a lace foamed petticoat) packed a powerful punch. Those allegedly respectable Victorians knew their eroticism all right.

The publicly decorous shoe (*i.e.* a sturdy, laced-up, little boot) was in fashion even in 1910. But the winds of fashion change were about to erupt into a hurricane.

As we have already seen, wars turn Fashion on its head — or heels! So World War I brought major changes that opened a latter day Pandora's Box, releasing startling and disturbing new ideas — and fashions. These exploded onto the social scene and things haven't been the same since.

In the early nineteen twenties (as fashion historian James Laver points out),[29] for the first time in civilized history women began to *expose their legs!* Skirts shrank to knee length and shook-up society on both sides of the Atlantic. Looking back from the vantage point of the miniskirt, it may be hard for us to imagine the impact of Flapper styles. What a visual bombshell!

The new short skirts were denounced by an alarmed clergy from every pulpit in western Europe. And in the U.S., several state legislatures proposed laws to prosecute "…any female over the age of fourteen who does not wear a skirt descending to that part of the body known as the instep."

But of course it didn't do any good. Women continued to kick-up their heels. And skirts continued to rise, right along with the stock market. In 1927, skirts reached a degree of elevation never seen before, with the result that shoes became a major component of fashion. High heels, with all their seductive messages, were here to stay.

The Twenties' high heels resemble nothing so much as a dancer's shoe — lighthearted, frivolous, with a shapely wineglass heel and a strap. And why not? Dancing shoes were a perfect symbol for this dizzy, speakeasy-going, high stepping era. This was the decade of *Our Dancing Daughters* (the 1928 film from MGM),[30] in which Joan Crawford's show- stopping Charleston said it all.

The Depression years, and on into the early Forties, saw high heels become sturdy pumps. They were the sensible older sisters to those Twenties' dancing shoes.

The end of World War II brought another milestone in shoe fashions. Christian Dior's New Look represented a very French interpretation of fashion. After wartime restrictions, his vision was as romantic as a morning shower on spring lilacs.

Women avidly embraced the New Look — the soft, feminine, elegant style that dictated tiny waists, flirtatious hats, full skirts with a *frou-frou* of petticoats. And the shoes! The femininity, luxury and downright gaiety of the times was epitomized by shoe designer Ferragamo's 1947 masterpiece. This surrealistic, almost invisible shoe was a bare sandal of transparent nylon threads on a curved, wedge heel.

But the real heel honcho of the postwar era was Roger Vivier, the designer who created the stiletto heel. His designs were fantasies, shoes with graceful, pointed toes and the thinnest, most elegant high heels ever seen. *Vogue* editor Diana Vreeland described a collection of his shoes that were featured in an exhibition at The Met as "...shoes made entirely of tulle, shoes of hummingbird feathers, shoes embroidered with tiny black pearls and coral, all with exquisite heels of lacquer."[31]

I have seen some of Vivier's footwear fantasies and they are extraordinary, almost enchanted. One could imagine them playing a leading role in a fairy tale. For example, those stiletto pumps decorated with black pearls and coral might well have graced the tortured feet of *The Little Mermaid,* in Hans Christian Andersen's classic tale.

And here we see another universal theme expressed through women's shoes.

In fairy tales, shoes are often used as symbols of a woman's sexual awakening and/or sexual fulfillment. In one story, *The Red Shoes*,[32] this sexual awareness is evil, dangerous, and ultimately fatal. (Those early storytellers really knew how to keep women in line.) Here, an evil shoemaker creates a pair of enchanted red shoes, and the hapless heroine comes under their spell. She puts on the shoes and dances away from her fiancé, her village, her safe and stable life. She cannot stop dancing and ultimately dances herself to death.

Wow! Quite a price to pay. But the implications are clear. Women must be very circumspect because their sexuality, once unleashed, is insatiable and uncontrollable. (Sounds to me like a girl who would never sit home on Saturday nights!)

The Red Heels is a contemporary fairy tale based on early New England legend and lore. In this tale, an itinerant shoemaker meets a mysterious young woman who asks him to make her a pair of new shoes. "From a wooden chest she pulled out a pair of dainty, but over-worn shoes....curiously, the carved wooden heels painted with red lacquer, seemed brand new. 'These heels are sturdy but cry out to be affixed to new shoes,' she said."[33] Jonathan smiled and nodded, but his heart sank at the sight of the crimson heels. "He had often heard country goodwives say that such heels were the sign of a witch."[34]

And the goodwives were right! The red heels are truly enchanted and the mysterious young woman is a witch — but a good, romantic one-man-woman type of witch. So she and Jonathan *dance* happily ever after.

Cinderella is the original "happily ever after" girl. In her story, it's sexual compatibility that's implied by the perfectly-fitting glass slipper. Incidentally, I think it's no coincidence that *Cinderella* is a French story. Is she going to suffer for her sexual awareness? *Mais non!* The practical French are totally approving of this clever girl who used her head and her dainty feet to step out of the scullery-kitchen and up into the Palace. Bravo!

By contrast, in *The Little Mermaid*, a woman pays dearly for sexual awakening and awareness.

You remember how it goes — once upon a time, when a little mermaid falls in love with a prince, a witch creates a spell that replaces the mermaid's tail with shapely legs and delicate feet. Now she can meet the prince, dance for him, and love him. But her joy is shattered with her first tentative step. As the witch had told her, "Everyone who sees you will say that you are the loveliest girl they have ever seen. But though you will move with a dancer's grace, every step you take will be like treading on a sharp knife-blade that cuts to the bone."[35]

(If you've ever worn a pair of very high heels to a dance, you can probably empathize.)

Enchanted shoes are not a new idea for the movies. Who can forget those sparkling little red pumps that transported Dorothy back to Kansas and all that was safe and sane and familiar. (This is the only example I have been able to discover where red shoes are innocent and sexless.)

Hang-Ups, The Secret Life of Clothes

Not so the leading role in *The Red Shoe Diaries*.[36] This is a sizzling series of triple X-rated movies wherein (so I'm told) the heroines wear red shoes — and often little else.

The quintessential red shoe message is seen in the movie *Summertime*.[37] In this classic Kate Hepburn "two hankie" movie, we see high heeled red shoes as a symbol of joyful sexual awakening, forget-tomorrow -passion, dance-the-night-away romance.

Here's the story (in case you've never seen it). It's summertime in Venice, and spinsterish school teacher Kate arrives for a once in a lifetime vacation. The city seems to envelop her in its romantic spell. And as if it had been penciled in by a good-witch travel agent, she meets and falls for Rossano Brazzi. He's darkly handsome, charming, intense. And he's crazy about her.

But there are complications. He's married, (though it's the usual European arrangement). She buys some antiques from him, then feels betrayed when they appear to be fakes. (But no, he explains everything.) There are more misunderstandings, but eventually, the electricity between them wins out and they make a date for a special evening.

In the next scene, we see Hepburn doing the Cinderella makeover bit. We are treated to a montage of Kate in a fashionable Venetian beauty salon — hair, make-up, manicure, pedicure. The Works! She emerges from the salon, radiant and a little breathless. Glowing with newfound confidence, she hurries along the arched corridor lined with shops. And then she sees them in a shop window — the red shoes!

The camera pans in for a close-up so we'll really get the message. These are the classic embodiment of sexual awakening: high heeled slides. *Red*. And designed with a clever flair that creates two symbolic little wings on the toe of each shoe. Little wings to carry her away....

Kate rushes to meet Rossano. She's wearing bare-shouldered black. The red heels click, click, clicking as she hurries along. They meet and the orchestra plays "their" song. They dance, they kiss. They stroll through dark Venetian streets and cross mysterious bridges. We see that she's carrying the red shoes. Now barefoot, the repressed spinster is gone forever and The Elemental Woman is freed at last.

As they move dreamily across a terrace to his apartment and slowly close the doors, fireworks light up the sky. And again, the camera zooms in to give us a final close-up of the red shoes, topsy-turvy on the weathered stones of the terrace. Do the lovers live happily ever after? Well, it's not a fairy-tale, in spite of the red shoes. You'll just have to rent the movie to see the bittersweet ending.

So much for the *visual* allure of high heels. But what about our other senses? High heels push our buttons with a double whammy. They appeal not only to the eyes, but to the ears with a sensual impact that I call audio allure.

Think about it. One of the most delicious aspects of high heels is the *sound* — the flirty, playful, coquettish click, click, click of high heels is unmistakable. And it's a sound that charms not only the listener but also the wearer of high heels. A woman wearing high heels becomes conscious of creating her own provocative background music for any drama that may unfold.

Here are some other examples of audio allure: the soft clitter-clatter of an armful of bangle bracelets, the rustle of taffeta, the delicate tinkling of a bell-laden ankle bracelet. One man, writing in *Esquire*, revealed that of all the erotic and exciting things in the world, the swoosh-swoosh sound of his ladylove's nylon-clad thighs rubbing against each other as she walked was the ultimate turn-on.

The impact of audio allure has been a major element in movies since the advent of sound.

If you're a truly dedicated movie-buff, you probably (as I do) sit in the still-darkened theatre long after the final "THE END" shot. The theme rises in volume and the complexities of making a movie unroll before you. *The Credits!* After the Producer, the Associate Producer (someone's brother-in-law), the Director, the Stars, the Cast, assorted camera people, hair stylists, the Chief Grip, etc., you'll always see a mysterious credit line... the Foley artist.

Now what in the world is a Foley artist? And what does this have to do with high heels? To get the answers to these questions, I interviewed two of the film industry's top sound experts: sound editor Pat Jackson (*The English Patient*[38] and *Amadeus*,[39] among countless credits) and Foley artist Denny Thorpe (*Bugsy*,[40] *102 Dalmatians*,[41] *The Mexican*[42] ...and more).

They explained that in the earliest "talkies," the actors were forced to be "can't walk and talk at the same time" robots. Because the crude sound systems of that era picked up *everything*, the actors' movements had to be very restricted. Then when they would move, the incidental sounds — the rustling of clothing, teacups on saucers, footsteps — overloaded the crude sound systems. (Note: the sound challenges of the first "talkies" are depicted hilariously in the fun-loving *Singin' in the Rain*.[43])

Fortunately, sound systems improved over time, and as Jackson explained, "directors could add the powerful impact of incidental sound, with all of its dramatic elements." Films could be both *movies* and *talkies*, and the actors could now move and talk at the same time. (Admittedly, a major challenge for some.)

Enter Mr. Foley. Yes, Virginia, there really was a Mr. Foley, a talented sound-technician who was uniquely sensitive to the dramatic impact and subtle nuances of incidental sound. It's true that directors and sound editors recognized that incidental sound could create a mood, intensify emotions and add layers of subtle meaning. But it was Foley who perfected the existing techniques and developed complex refinements.

For example, he realized that it wasn't enough to simply add the sound of footsteps in a dramatic scene. If the sound was one dimensional, or if it was not a true audio representation, dramatic impact and authenticity were lost. So if a scene called for a detective to walk down the corridor of a cheap hotel, Foley believed that those footsteps had to sound like heels on *cheap linoleum*, and not the echoes of footfalls on cement or marble or even polished wood. (And if it was a seedy detective, the shoes should squeak!)

He set up a special studio where there were a hundred different surfaces—gravel, linoleum (cheap and quality!), metal (think tenement fire escapes), carpets, wooden floors (creaky and otherwise), and on and on. These 6' by 6' surfaces are still called "Foley Pits" and the sound technicians called "Foley artists."

And they truly are artists. Pat Jackson explained that technical advances have made it possible to move to subtler and subtler layers of sound, each layer able to create dramatic dimensions not even dreamed of in earlier productions.

This example from *The English Patient*[44] will illustrate. "When we started editing the sound on 'Patient'" Jackson told me, "we realized that the footsteps throughout were too crisp and clear — not right at all. Then director Anthony Minghella said, 'They're in North Africa, for God's sake! *Everything* would be covered with a layer of grit.' So that's just what we had the Foley artist do — cover that

Foley pit with a layer of gritty dust and then re-record all footsteps with this added element."

And if you've seen this elegant film, you know that it's a masterpiece because of such exquisite detail.

Of course, incidental sound involves all kinds of audio-detail, not just foot steps. (Foley artist Thorpe has items in her collection that will even create the evocative, luxurious sound of a mink coat. Amazing!)

But high heels are a favorite challenge for Foley artists. The audio nuances of high heeled shoes are so wide ranging that Thorpe has 300 pair in her Foley repertoire. "In *102 Dalmatians*, we needed the sound of evil, power stilettos. I used one of the favorites in my collection, a pair of leopard-skin ultra high heeled 'killers'." Pat Jackson told me these shoes are famous in the industry. "They absolutely *sound* wicked!"

Thorpe went on to say, "The sound of high heels can say lots of things, not only sexy, but defiant, angry, or even discouraged. The sound of high heels, scuffing along, is a really defeated sound." She adds that some current styles, with their heavy, unyielding plastic soles, "…make a sound that's so different, it's almost offensive."

However, a contemporary shoe style that she does like is one that she used for Julia Roberts in *The Mexican*. "Julia wore these little slides…you know, the kind that have about 2" heels. This heel height means that the shoe slaps back at the sole after every step, making a wonderful little

Hang-Ups, The Secret Life of Clothes

duet to the sound of the heels. It's kind of like the sound of applause. With every step, these shoes are saying, 'Baby, you're the BEST!'"

She added, "The sound of the stiletto heel is tappier than any other. And as the name 'stiletto' implies, that 'click, click, click' will cut through any other sounds that are going on in a scene — even the sound of a jackhammer!"

Perhaps that's the ultimate appeal of high heels. On some deep level, every woman recognizes that the staccato call of high-rise heels is like a sexual beeper.

Click, click, click your way past any big city construction site and you'll see what I mean. Those bronzed hunks will look up from machine, power-saw or hammer — possibly to whistle, perhaps to shout. Certainly to check out the source of that irresistibly intriguing sound — a woman's high heels.

5

When the Going Gets Tough

When the Going Gets Tough

*A*merica has fought many wars, and for each one there has been a defining rallying cry, a call to arms.

"The British are coming, the British are coming...." mobilized the first Americans. *"Uncle Sam wants you!"* motivated thousands to become doughboys and fight "Over There" in WWI.

"Remember Pearl Harbor" had a rich and lusty ring and was a fierce reminder of the betrayal that ushered in WWII. It worked, too — inspiring Americans to join up, plant Victory gardens, and stoically accept rationing. And America's women were motivated to bundle their long "Rita Hayworth manes" into a hair-net Snood, pick up a rivet gun and report to the local defense plant.

Today, after Nine-One-One, we again find ourselves at war. And our President has issued the latest call to arms. Looking earnestly into the camera, that good man has uttered the rallying cry of Nine-One-One: ***"Go shopping!"*** In speech after speech, he has urged astonished Americans to "...go out to the malls and *go shopping*."

The initial reaction to this directive was that it was an impossibly bizarre response from any leader whose country had been viciously attacked. But of course, upon reflection, all those wise analysts and "talking heads" on the Sunday shows soon agreed that it was a sensible stance, designed to be an antidote for one of our gravest challenges, the slumping U.S. economy.

But wait! Have the political pundits got it wrong? Is it only the economy that motivates this insistent message? Or have we all, once again, underestimated Mr. Bush? Perhaps, underneath that tough, tongue-tangled Texas veneer lives a wise-as-Solomon leader.

Looking out at his countrymen (and *women)* who are reeling under the trauma of war, he has recognized that we need therapy, the kind of encompassing, comforting therapy that can only be delivered by a truly satisfying shopping spree. Sort of credit card Prozac. Yes, I think he's a very wise and inspired leader. (Who knew?) And let's remember that we're talking Texas here. Those Neiman Marcus roots run wide and deep.

The President may even have had a secret committee studying those tongue-in-chic, prescient bumper stickers: "I shop, therefore I am," "To shop is to live" and for those who OD on the experience, "Stop me, before I shop again!"

I know you think I'm exaggerating. But President Bush and I aren't the only ones to recognize the profound impact a shopping trip can have on the human psyche.

You may be surprised to learn that for some very famous people, a shopping trip has been an antidote for grief and loss. Joan Rivers, for example. In an in-depth TV biography, she told Barbara Walters about the traumatic experience of her husband Edgar's suicide. She recalled that it had come as a total shock. As with most suicides, those closest to the person seem to have no idea of the totality of their depression. "I was in New York when I got the phone call," she told Walters.

"What was your very first reaction?" (Leaning forward, Walters is like a terrier digging for the emotional Mother Lode....) "Of course, I immediately called our daughter Melissa." Remembering, Rivers' lip trembles. "And we got together and went shopping."

Shopping! Barbara was visibly shocked. But Joan went on to explain that this was a pleasurable activity that she and her daughter often shared, and that Edgar had loved the idea that they *could* shop and be extravagant. For Rivers and her daughter, it was a statement of continuity and confidence. Listening to Joan, that certainly made sense.

Shopping was part of grief therapy for another famous woman, Jackie Kennedy Onassis. In her book *Great Dames*,[45] author Marie Brenner recalls seeing a video news clip showing Jackie and her sister Lee Radziwill, shortly after their mother's funeral. They were strolling arm-in-arm along *Avenue Montaigne* in Paris, on a major shopping spree. Instead of condemning them for being shallow or unfeeling, here's Brenner's "take" on the story....

"I felt it sent a message, 'Never waste a moment!'" She went on to speculate that perhaps their mother's death made the sisters realize the fragility of Life. Maybe this was an opportunity for them to mend some emotional fences, damaged by sibling rivalry.

But I interpreted the story in a different way. Perhaps they were recalling childhood shopping trips in Paris with their mother, special trips wherein they would feel very grown up and secure — for a while, at least — in their privileged world.

(The reality of their early years, according to biographers, is that their position was often very insecure. Dashing "Black Jack" Bouvier was neither a husband nor father who could be depended upon for emotional or financial support.)

I found myself remembering shopping trips with my own mother, the warm feeling of almost conspiratorial companionship, and those gentle lessons in taste and discernment. ("Polka dots? Hmm!! Let's see how this darling plaid looks first." "Do you see that this blue isn't *quite* the same shade as turquoise?") And so on. The afternoon would be completed, multi-bags in hand, with a "Ladies" lunch at the Bullock's Wilshire tea room. Yes, I could certainly understand Joan and Jackie's shopping therapy.

Shopping not only comforts the heart, it warms the heart, too. Plenty!

All those mega-millionaires who take their "Diamonds are a Girl's Best Friend"[46] companions for an evening junket to Tiffany's (to be followed by a little late supper) have long recognized that a pleasant hour spent shopping for some charming baubles creates in their golden girlfriends a rush of affection and a miraculous personal makeover. Suddenly, Mr. Rich becomes Mr. Handsome: tall (so what if he's standing on his wallet), debonaire, irresistible.

For William Randolph Hearst and Marion Davies, the "treatment" was effective and their liaison permanent, even though Hearst seemed to be the perennial suitor ever trying to ensure his conquest of a lukewarm lover with sparkling, gleaming enticements.

But their story has a heart warming ending that just shows how effective all that shopping was. Toward the end of Hearst's life, when he was facing a serious financial crisis, Davies not only stuck with him, she sold her vast collection of jewels to pay off his creditors.

Elements of the Hearst story illustrate that shopping may be at the core of that famous advice, "Living well is the best revenge." According to inner circle gossip, Mrs. William Randolph Hearst was humiliated by the scandal of her husband's very public affair. When the first revealing photos were published, she soothed her pain with a trip to her favorite Fifth Avenue jeweler, and walked out with a comforting purchase — a string of flawless pearls that cost a jolting six-figures.

Sliding that lavish, lustrous strand around her neck was probably as soothing as any sedative or antidepressant. Rich as Hearst was, Millicent knew that the extravagant purchase would be galling to him, and she wore those spectacular pearls on every possible occasion.

But you don't have to look to celebrities and millionaires to find examples of the therapy of shopping. You just might find an example or two in your very own closet.

The truth is, shopping can deliver a deeply satisfying, embracing experience that touches us on many levels — the visual "hit" of a stunningly original window display, the lights, the music (subliminally loaded, for all we know), the perfumes and scented air. And the enchantment of seeing ourselves in an entirely new way as we view our up-to-the-minute reflection in the mirrors of Sak's or "Bloomie's".

An important part of this experience is the professional saleswoman. As rare today as a well-groomed teenager, you may still find one in the most exclusive designer departments of the best department stores, or in a special boutique where personal attention is the stock-in-trade (and every sale counts!).

It's here that the shopping experience becomes visceral, a mind altering "trip" that explains the need for those twelve-step Shopaholic support groups. It's here, in this charming little boutique, that we meet the skilled manipulator who assures us: *"No one has been able to carry-off this red satin jumpsuit the way you have."*

Eyeing our reflection, we suspect that she's lying.

"Maggie, come over here," the saleswoman calls to her cohort. *"Look at this Red on Mrs. B——. Remember, I told you no one would be able to carry off this Look? Well, I was wrong…"* And an aside to you:

> *"Karan always designs for that special, daring woman…"*

Yes, she's definitely lying. But we don't care. Anymore than the tired business man, completing his sexual encounter with some siliconed escort girl, believes her when she whispers: *"That's the most fantastic sex I've ever experienced."* It just feels good to hear the lie. Self-deception isn't part of the equation. And while we may not buy the lie — and the jumpsuit that goes with it — we will surely walk out with some of the more believable fantasies.

Reading this, you may feel (smugly?) that you are immune to such blandishments. But be honest now. What woman hasn't spent an hour (and a few hundred bucks) in some unique little shop, wondering at her reflection in the flattering light and viewing herself in a new role. (*"Why haven't I ever worn black coq feathers before? They're <u>me!</u>"*) Warmed by a glass or two of white wine, with compliments swirling about her head, how wonderful it is to forget the challenges and grey truths of one's life. To forget perhaps, selfish, demanding children, an indifferent husband, or a mind-numbing job.

In those shared moments with our most private Self reflected in the magic mirror, we see a new *persona*, a fascinating newly discovered entity. And anything seems possible. Sometimes the magic is so strong, a woman needs superhuman willpower not to drop-in at the travel agency next door, boutique bags in hand, to book a one-way ticket to Rio.

Yes, shopping can be a "trip," but there are several categories. They're not all voyages into a fantasy of potential life scripts.

For some, shopping is the ultimate sport. And in the same way that Hemingway traveled the world, seeking the premier hunting experience, the true Sport Shopper studies the terrain and knows the best hunting preserves, from Loehmann's to Filene's basement — with side trips to Pier One, the Museum Shop in the Metropolitan or Getty, and consignment shops (*depots-vente*) on the Right Bank.

Then there's the local terrain — the best department store or specialty shop in your own home town. This is where you see the true Sport Shoppers, modern Diana's armed with credit cards, stalking the trophy bargain. Qualifiers are any item of couture design or luxurious fabric, marked down once, twice, *three* times. Now that's a trophy tag worthy of framing!

The dedicated Sport Shopper wouldn't think of "buying in" to those pretend bargain centers, the Discount Cluster at the edge of the freeway. She knows her prey and the terrain and recognizes that (even though the signs say *Calvin Klein, Coach, DKNY, Joan and David*) so much of the merchandise in that gaggle of roadside buildings will be off-season, off-market, and off-color — bland and uninteresting department store rejects.

The real thrills come from purchases in those unexpected little shops just off Madison Avenue, at the far end of Melrose, or down a *petite allee* off the *rue du Fau*. These shops are usually stark, dark, the size of a closet, and manned by enigmatic salespeople who leave you alone to make your discoveries.

It is here that you can find the most amazing treasures — soft-as-butter Italian suede boots in one; chic, unmatronly cashmere sweaters in another. Here you'll find unique handbags guaranteed to impress haughty *maitre d*'s, and cleverly designed jackets that will become wardrobe favorites. All at not-to-be-believed prices.

But when you return to one of these treasure troves to repeat your triumphant purchases, more often than not the little shop has disappeared, leaving only a tattered, handwritten notice taped to the window as proof that it existed at all.

Where do they come from and where do they go, these bargain bazaars? Frankly, it's best not to think about it, and to avoid reading certain back page newspaper stories such as "Police Baffled by Retail Hijacker Ring."

Shopping *a la chasse* has no relationship to those sporting dilettantes (usually "Ladies Who Lunch" types) who stroll into the designer salons of Bergdorf's or Neiman's on the first day of a privately- advertised "Select Merchandise Reduced" sale, and bag the prizes.

To the true Sport Shopper, this is equivalent to a maharajah's hunting charade wherein the hapless prey is enclosed in a restricted area, to be flushed out by native beaters and dropped by as many shots as it takes. By contrast, the Sport Shopper knows the real thrill of the hunt. That wild shopping terrain in the malls of New Jersey, for example, where shopping is ruthless, narrow eyed, smash-and-grab sport.

There are those who say you should always do serious shopping alone. And I agree. The results of shopping with a girlfriend are too often a wasted afternoon, a fattening lunch, and bags of ill-advised purchases, the consequence of being egged on by a loyal friend. *"No, those pants really, really don't make you look fat. And look at the price!"*

Certainly, shopping for basics is also a solo event. The straight black skirt or beige pantyhose or gray sweatpants shopping chore is something like a trip to the dentist, a necessary task to complete with as much dispatch as possible.

Hang-Ups, The Secret Life of Clothes

When you need some important, crucial item of clothing — something to wear to your ex's funeral, for example — go alone. Don't go with a girl chum. And for heaven's sake, don't go with The Man In Your Life. (Are you crazy?) If you want to nurture the romance in your relationship, I'd also avoid taking him with you when you are shopping for something deadly practical — flannel sheets, walking shoes, white cotton *anything*.

A man and a woman shopping together is an opportunity to create a memory — for him, the fantasy of being a tanned Greek shipping magnate, lavishing largesse on his trophy woman. For her, the delicious experience of being pampered and indulged and precious…the full focus of all his admiring attentions. (With perhaps a dispensation for his few bantering remarks with the attractive salesgirl.)

Yes, shopping can nurture and fuel any romance. And it doesn't have to involve black lace.

Even shopping for a woman's gray flannel suit can be erotically charged, as Alfred Hitchcock demonstrated in *Vertigo*.[47] No doubt you've seen this movie many times. (It certainly deserves that overworked adjective, *classic*.) But I think you'll enjoy this unique insight into the pivotal shopping scenes. This is how the story goes.…

In *Vertigo's* convoluted plot, Jimmy Stewart is Scotty Ferguson, a retired San Francisco Police detective. An old friend, Gavin Elster (character actor Tom Helmore) dupes him into playing an essential role in an elaborate murder scheme.

Elster asks the detective to "shadow" his wife Madeline because he fears for her safety and sanity. According to the concerned husband, she has become neurotic, suicidal, possibly mad. Perhaps Stewart can unravel the mystery of her wanderings through San Francisco's most dramatically photogenic sites. He may even be instrumental in saving her life. Noble nice guy that he is, Stewart can't refuse the job. And when he gets a look at Madeline (blonde screen goddess Kim Novak), his goose is cooked so to speak.

The hidden agenda is for Novak (who is really Gavin's mistress) to enchant Stewart and make him fall in love with her. Then, when the husband murders his wife, Stewart will be witness to what he *thinks* is the reality — namely, that it is Madeline who makes a suicidal plunge to her death. In fact, it is the real wife who is substituted for Madeline at the last minute. (Are you with me, so far?)

As the murderous husband had planned, the plot comes off without a hitch, and Stewart is a convincing witness to the wife's supposed suicide. After the funeral, the husband leaves for Europe and the detective tries to resume his normal life. But he is shattered by Madeline's apparent death and his obsession with the blonde goddess persists.

As he wanders the same San Francisco haunts where he had first seen Madeline, every blonde woman becomes a potential resurrection of his lost love. But one day, while walking along Post Street, a beautiful brunette catches his eye. She's flashy, sexy — but there's something more. Yes. That's it! She reminds him of Madeline.

Which is not surprising. We, the audience, know that the brunette Judy Barton, *is* in fact Madeline. (Both roles played by Kim Novak.) We also know that, in the midst of the elaborate murder plot, she has fallen in love with the detective.

So these are the dramatic undercurrents just below the surface of the intriguing shopping scenes. After their meeting on the street, Judy and the detective go out — to all the same places where Stewart had first seen Madeline. But somehow, being with Judy doesn't fill the emptiness left by Madeline. If Judy were just a bit different — more elegant, perhaps blonde. Hmm!!. Stewart says to her, "Judy, I want to take care of you… I want to buy you nice things…" And so, he and a reluctant Judy go shopping.

In the elegant Ransohoff's Designer Salon, Stewart is like a man possessed, instructing the attentive saleswoman to find the *exact* grey flannel suit, the *identical* classic pumps, that Madeline had worn. As Scotty progresses with her makeover, the erotic impact of Judy's metamorphosis is unique. It is a lover's striptease in reverse. Instead of the seduction growing with the removal of clothing, the eroticism intensifies with each additional clothing purchase.

Hitchcock himself explained the concept. "Cinematically, all of Stewart's efforts to recreate the dead woman are shown in such a way that he seems to be trying to undress her, instead of the other way around."[48]

It's sort of fashion as foreplay. The sexual tension builds to a climax when they return to Judy's apartment, after she's had her hair bleached blonde. There she stands, in her grey "Madeline" suit, her classic pumps, her newly blonde hair. Her eyes are filled with love and desire for the detective, but still he's disappointed. The illusion is not complete. Novak hasn't twisted her hair up into the elegant bun that Madeline wore. According to Hitchcock: " What this really means is that the girl has almost stripped, but she still won't take her knickers off."[49] Stewart asks her to change her hair, to pin it up. But she protests. Finally she says, "Oh, all right!" and goes into the bathroom.

Stewart waits for her eagerly, breathlessly. "What he is really waiting for," Hitchcock continued, "— is for the woman to emerge — totally naked this time and ready for love."[50]

And she does. Emerge, I mean. But of course, she's fully clothed in all the things they had shopped for. And, finally, she's the exact image of Madeline. Stewart is overcome with desire by the vision he has created — the classic grey suit, the elegant shoes, the severe hair style. He sweeps her into a passionate embrace. They kiss and kiss. (Hey there, Mr. Stewart!)

Yes, shopping can make a real contribution to your love life — but I don't think that's what our president had in mind when he urged us to get out and about and "go to the malls." Surely, he was again revealing his unique understanding of human nature.

"*To the Malls*" is a battle cry that's right on the money, no doubt intended to remind us of our oneness as a people and to give us a unifying sense of community.

After all, from the dawn of history, the marketplace has served as a concentrating hub, a nucleus of culture and an energizing center for human activities of all kinds. Ask any archeologist of your acquaintance and she'll tell you that discovering the market place of an ancient people is a bonanza. So many aspects of that remote culture — the diet, clothes, sports, social and sexual customs — will be revealed in the market place discovery at some remote "dig." (And, who knows? Maybe the mysterious hieroglyphs on an ancient chard will ultimately translate out to read: "All sales final…")

But it's not only ancient peoples who have used the market place as an energizing event in otherwise hum-drum lives. People all over the world, from Oaxaca to Prague to Birmingham, make market day an *event*.

I witnessed a charming illustration of this phenomenon in a little village in West Sussex. My then-husband and I were tramping around rural England on a writing assignment. We had decided to stay at a Bed and Breakfast place on the outskirts of a small town.

This B & B wasn't an inn or lodge, but really just a farmhouse where the *very* nice farm family, wanting to make a few extra pounds, rented out their spare room to travelers. We had stayed one night, slept in a bit, and been served a full English breakfast. But on the second night, the farmer's wife asked us if we would mind being up and about (and out) before eight a.m. the next morning. We were glad to oblige, since we wanted to get on with our trek.

The next morning we arose, quickly dressed, and went into the farm kitchen. And there was the entire family — children, polished and shining in short pants (for him) and a flowered frock (for her). Mister Farmer was wearing a suit (brown, of course) *and* a vest. And Madam Farmer was wearing a flowered dress and a fully flowered hat.

Dear God, I thought. Someone has died and we've imposed on this sweet family when they are preparing to go to a funeral. But no. Everyone was so cheery — really in a holiday mood. And then, the mystery was solved when Madam Farmer said: "*I do apologize for routing you out so early. It's Market Day, you know.*"

Market Day! In this tiny unprepossessing village, this was a gala event, requiring special clothes and advance planning. These were such simple and good people. It seemed quite wonderful that they made their Market Day such an occasion.

In the ensuing years since that morning in West Sussex, I have come to recognize that Market Day (or its equivalent) is an event all over the world. Indeed, the market place provides a sense of community and connection as no other human activity can. While moralists may decry the materialism of our own society, the truth is, whether in Hong Kong or Cincinnati, Lyon or Casablanca, the market place is where it's at.

Take the marketplace at Intawella, for example. (It's the one in North Africa, on the outskirts of the Sahara Desert.) Have you been there? Neither have I. But I go there often in my imagination, via the pages of a well-thumbed coffee-table book, *Nomads of Niger*.[51] In this book, author/anthropologist Marion Van Offel chronicles the lives of the Wodaabe, the last nomadic people on earth.

What captures me, and takes me to these pages again and again is the *mardi gras* aspect of their quarterly pageant to their "market town" — the marketplace at Intawella.

Here, in the bleakest countryside on the face of the earth, surrounded by the parched brown vistas of the Sahara, these nomadic people present a glamourous, visu-ally-sophisticated image that is extraordinary.

Photographer Carol Beckwith has captured countless arresting images of these stunning people as the nomads gather at Intawella to sell and trade — goats, cattle, salt, spices. And the finery! Gleaming brass bracelets and ear-rings, lengths of brocade, ribbons flashed with gold. It's here at the market place that the young men eye the young girls. Where the young girls giggle and chatter and eye the young men. Where the grandmothers trade herbal wisdom and theories of child rearing. And the men tell tall tales of battles and sport. In a word, it's much like your local mall.

Author Van Offel tells us that each trip to the market event requires a creative change of clothes to match that holiday mood. (Just like in West Sussex.) She describes the preparations of one family:

"Mokao changes his worn, everyday clothing for a sky blue tunic and a loose, sleeveless robe of the same color. With great care, he wraps a white turban around his head. For her part, Mowa puts a beautiful indigo colored cloth around her everyday wrapper..."[52]

Then, they load the donkeys and off they go to Intawella!

It's very clear. Whether a farm family in rural England or a nomadic family from Niger, there is an endearing sameness to the human experience. And whether we call them market places or bazaars or malls, the unifying concept is the same.

Nevertheless, in some circles, its very fashionable to disdain shopping at the mall. We all have at least one friend who will tell us of her shopping *Angst*. "My *dear, I couldn't find it anywhere but at the* Mall," she will complain to you (...Marie Antoinette, struggling against the necessity of confronting the mob...).

Perhaps now, you'll have a different perspective on her posturing. You'll know that your condescending friend, with her sojourn at the marketplace, has had to join the human race. And let me share with you her dirty little secret. Given that over a *billion* shoppers visit America's malls in peak months, she's no doubt shopped there *often*, just like the rest of us.

(In fact, I'd be willing to bet she's been to the local mall so many times, she even knows where the bathrooms are!)

Shopping — whether it enhances our dreams or supports our sense of community — is an important element in the human experience. But should shopping be used as a concerted part of a war effort? I'll leave it to you to decide. One thing is sure. We haven't heard the last of this shop for victory effort.

Just yesterday when I was shopping at The Mall (and yes, I know where the bathrooms are...), I saw a clever new thrust in this "Shop 'til *they* drop" campaign. Every store window displayed a simple poster that carried a powerful visual message. The poster consisted of the flag with two handles at the top, thus turning the Stars and Stripes into a giant, patriotic shopping bag.

At this writing, the war news is positive. Still, the President has warned us that the war on terrorism may be a lengthy one. (Everyone in Washington seems to think so, too.) And as the battles drag on, we can expect President Bush to continue his strong leadership.

Do you remember, in those first weeks after the Nine-One-One attack, how he gave us regular briefings and inspiring words of encouragement? We can expect more of the same if things get increasingly "dicey."

Yes, I see it now. Another Oval Office speech. Our President, in a voice filled with resolve, recalls our brave heritage — the Pilgrims, the Pioneers, the Greatest Generation. His message: *"Be brave, stay the course,"* comes to a thrilling conclusion. Looking into the TV camera, eyes steady, jaw firm, he calls us to our own greatness...

> *"And remember, my fellow Americans, when the going gets tough, the tough go shopping!"*

6

Black
and a
Jacket

Black and a Jacket

*J*ust across from the Chanel building, on *Avenue Montaigne*, there's a restaurant called *l'Avenue*. In spite of the fleeting nature of restaurant popularity, it remains one of the most "In" places in Paris, a luncheon rendez-vous for film people, corporate big-wigs, the media and other *cognoscenti*. It was very crowded on this early autumn afternoon, but since my companion was a member in good standing of one of these rarified worlds, we were quickly shown to an "A List" table in the preferred upstairs dining room.

The serving people — one could hardly call them waiters — were without exception, young would-be models and actors of devastating beauty. A languid Naomi Campbell look-alike handed menus around and we became engrossed in the *really* important part of any Parisian interaction — the food. After much discussion and an extended debate over the wine, lunch was underway.

As I looked around the elegant room, enjoying the panorama of assorted and easily recognizable types, my companion called to my attention a small table set in front of tall French windows. He told me that the two distinguished looking men sitting there were leading figures in the French government — the current Minister of Finance and the former financial Minister. Yes, I was impressed. And I studied them closely as they engaged in animated conversation. Was there any indication of *malaise* or stress in their body language? Was there the slightest hint of dyspepsia that might foreshadow an international financial crisis? Would the Euro plunge and the *franc* re-emerge?

No, they were obviously enjoying their food, their wine, and their conversation. I relaxed and returned my cell phone to its case. (There was no need to call my broker.) I concentrated on my excellent *saumon* and the superb wine. When I looked back at the window table, I saw that the two men had been replaced by two women. No, let me rather say, two *Parisiennes*. These were quintessential French women, of a certain age and such formidable flair, if you met them on Mars you'd know they were just taking a break from strolls along the *Champs Elysées*.

Thin, intense, leaning forward with the air of two conspirators, their rather flat, high cheek-boned faces were animated. Both of them were smoking and they used their cigarettes to add dramatic emphasis to whatever words were being said, now pulling smoke voraciously into their lungs, or expelling a perfect plume of smoke through gleaming, pouted lips. Their slender white hands, sparkling with jewels, the fingers tipped in scarlet, swirled cigarette chemtrails with each eloquent Gallic gesture.

What a dramatic picture they made, their chiseled profiles and sleek hair wreathed in veils of backlit smoke. It was an Irving Penn photograph brought to life. And what were they wearing, these icons of Style? You probably know the answer. They were wearing The Uniform — Black and a Jacket!

One of the women had chosen a jacket of unquestioned Couture lineage — Gucci, I thought — obvious in the richness and radiance of the poppy red fabric and the clever buttons. A strand of oversized Chanel pearls were a witty counterpoint to — what looked to be, at this distance — a black cotton t-shirt. (Let's hear it for the Gap!) Her companion was wearing a scaled down blazer in that bright blue that I always think of as Saint Laurent and maybe that was the label here. Anyway, it looked fabulous, closely fitted through the waist and unbuttoned just enough to show the black and blue nautical striped sweater underneath. Both women were wearing short black skirts and slender pumps with towering high heels.

Yes. They were wearing the uniform that takes a woman anywhere, anytime… beautifully, securely. I looked around the room to see other examples. And there were plenty. The redhead in a corner banquette was wearing an acid green jacket with exaggerated sleeves and oversized fringed cuffs. A Sonia Rykell from the back of the closet, I thought. But still timely and *chic*. A black silk shirt and black pants were the non-competing backdrop for this unusual garment.

Another stunning woman was sitting across from us. She was wearing a flawlessly tailored white tweed jacket, paired with a black silk sweater, cigarette pants and little black boots. It was a costume of perfect fashion pitch. (The important diamond pin at the shoulder didn't hurt at all.)

The truth is, you could travel the world in Black and a Jacket. It's a sartorial version of the salesman's line, "You can travel the world on a smile and a hand shake."

There is something so dependable about a jacket, like the friend you can call at three o'clock in the morning. A jacket is always there for you — staunch, trustworthy — not likely to embarrass you or leave you vulnerable to ridicule or prosecution by the Fashion Police. A jacket is the answer to "What shall I wear?", no matter what the circumstance.

But does that mean that jackets are as boring as your Aunt Betty? Not at all. They're more like your very own Auntie Mame, ever ready with an answer and an eye for undreamed of opportunities. For example, that black satin dinner jacket. Elegant and understated, it can become a sly conspirator that allows you to wear a transparent, Bad Girl camisole and still maintain a guileless, "Who, me?" demeanor in the face of come-ons or glares.

Or on a beach at St. Barts, when everyone else is barely there in bikinis and thongs and little else, you can toss a studded, oversized denim jacket over your black bikini and stand out with an image that's all tan legs and a sort of, "I'm not trying that hard" attitude. (And at the same time, you'll cover up a few pesky, cellulite secrets.)

As I've said, a jacket is the answer to what to wear, anytime, any place. The trick is to choose an interesting jacket, a jacket in a striking or meltingly flattering color, a jacket with a superb cut, rich or unexpected fabric, important buttons — in other words, a jacket with attitude. This is no place for a mild-mannered classic beige blazer. (Never send a boy to do a man's job!) And always, worn with the non-competing backdrop of basic black. (Oh, all right. All white would work, too. Or deep, chocolate brown.)

This combination is such sure fire flattery, you can bet that it's not new to Hollywood. In fact, it's an old Hollywood trick, devised by those gifted designers of the classic Hollywood eras who were challenged to flatter and disguise the figure problems of aging, reigning movie queens.

An all black background — a dress or clever jump suit or even just a black sweater and skirt — worn under a dramatically beautiful jacket (or even a coat, for those who need real help) was a visual sleight of hand that works its magic in reel or real life.

This design ploy has the effect of diminishing the figure underneath the jacket, making it almost disappear, so there's only the visual impact of glorious hair, a great face, terrific legs, graceful hands. And, if you can carry it off, a dynamite décolletage. (Note: this is an image formula well within the reach of many real life women.)

Jackets are so basic, so elemental, it's always surprising when the fashion press rediscovers them, which they do with cyclical regularity. For example, *Vogue* announced in March 2002: "The Newly Discovered Jacket!!!" That's kind of like saying, "Wow! Did you notice that big ball of fire on the horizon? Those 'in the know' are calling it The Sun!"

But look, fashion reporters have a tough time of it. They are required to come up with new, new, new breathless headlines every month.

Jackets are hardly new. Their antecedents go back as far as 1350. This period marked the appearance of the *houppelande*, or overcoat, a garment that was the first to sport a real collar. Coats and waistcoats (1710), cutaways and frock coats (1815), sack coats and vests (1850) — all are precursors of today's jackets.

You can see that the jacket has been an ongoing staple of men's wardrobes for centuries. It is and always has been a garment of authority and position, a symbolic mantle of power.

Jackets occupy a unique place in the symbolism of women's fashion, too. Dean of fashion historians James Laver has explained that the essential difference between men's and women's clothes is that "…women's clothes…are governed by what is called the Seduction Principle…men's clothes are governed by the Hierarchical Principle."[53] He goes on to say that the purpose of men's clothes is to make a clear statement of power and position, while women's clothes have been traditionally used as a means of enhancing sexual desirability and availability.

So the jacket in your closet represents something new. It clearly reveals the expanded role of women in contemporary society. It is a power garment, stolen from the male (as we shall see) and represents and supports the empowered roles that women play in today's world.

Most fashion historians agree that Chanel is the creator of the jacket as we know it today. How Chanel stole the Duke's blazer is part of her legend. And the story goes like this….

The fascinating Chanel had two great loves in her life, the Grand Duke Dmitri of Russia and England's Duke of Westminster (one of the premier peers of the realm). Not bad for a little peasant girl from murky and obscure origins in the South of France.

Diana Vreeland, who knew her well, described Chanel as "…mesmerizing, strange, alarming, witty….you can't compare anyone with Chanel."[54] Her love affair with the Englishman lasted six passionate years and during that time, according to Vreeland, "…she learned about afternoon teas….about magnificently maintained country houses…"[55] and the elegance and luxury of that aristocratic life. It was in this outdoor, sporting atmosphere that Chanel saw the clean, uncluttered turnout of Eton boys and men at shoots in their impeccable tweeds.

One can imagine her — that unique and daring *gamin* figure — borrowing the Duke's blazer on many cool afternoons and tossing it over her square shoulders. Or sliding into his brass buttoned blue flannel, an appealing picture of a little girl in Daddy's coat.

So this was the origin of the Chanel jacket — superbly tailored, brass-buttoned, impeccable and perfect. It was and is a garment designed to create for every woman a youthful, slightly athletic, energetic image. The square shoulders, subtly padded, have the effect of minimizing hips. The elongated proportion of the waist and the close fitting sleeves are visual sleights of hand that create lithe proportions where none may exist.

And the armholes! According to Vreeland, "Chanel was a nut on armholes! She was always snipping and taking out sleeves and driving the tailors absolutely crazy."[56] It will pay you to be a nut about armholes, too, because the fit of the sleeve at the underarm is a proportion that can make you look taller, more slender, lift your bust line, and just generally make you look terrific.

In fact, the magical set-in sleeve is one of the wonders of Western Civilization. If you sew at all, you know that the set-in sleeve is a miracle of sophisticated fabric sculpture, all that steaming and shaping and easing of a bell-shaped sleeve into a small circular armhole. It is definitely not easy! And when it's done correctly, *a la* Chanel, that sleeve will be set-in very high, close to your armpit — thereby creating a lithe and long line through your mid-section.

A jacket with a sloppy, bulky or just low-placed arm-hole will automatically make you look dumpy and (shud-der) a bit matronly. Am I overstating the case? Just try it. The next time you're shopping for a jacket, pay particular attention to the fit of the sleeve. And if the sleeve fits, wear it!

The Chanel jacket was so right, so perfect for the lifestyles of thousands of women, that it has been a main-stay of women's wardrobes for over seventy years. In fact, the Fall 2002 Chanel collection, designed by Karl Lagerfeld, was an *homage* to the original Chanel style and embodied all of the unique characteristics that created the legend.

However, the Chanel jacket has gone through many metamorphoses. After WWII, Chanel herself encouraged the knockoffs that appeared everywhere. The rumor was that she showed her collections to the copyists first, even before the formal show. What did she care? She had done it all and had achieved that position beyond success. She was an *icon*, permanently enshrined in the cultural history of the twentieth century and she wanted women every-where to share her vision.

Unfortunately, that superb Chanel image — jaunty, ever-young, slightly rebellious — segued through countless knockoffs into the ditsy little jacket of the Fifties. Supremely unflattering, this boxy garment accented every proportion that women would like to change. It ended at the fullest part of a woman's hips, with three-quarter sleeves adding even more visual width. These boxy, unfitted jackets resemble nothing so much as a pre-maternity jacket.

However, this unflattering image was both appropriate and significant. It truly reflected the mood of the times since every postwar era is a call to get back to home and hearth, and *reproduce*. In the United States, the Fifties was the final celebration and deification of the good little housewife and mother. Think Doris Day, and later, any daytime image of first lady Jacqueline Kennedy.

In the Sixties, as we all know, change — *big* change — was in the air. And the pendulum of fashion would swing way, way out into a crazy world of gypsies and vagabond's, wanderers and bikers. It was all wildly creative and free and undisciplined. Then, it was the morning-after. Surprise, surprise! Those charming wanderers were nowhere to be found. And women learned that they had to depend on themselves. It was time for a new costume to reflect the sobering change in women's consciousness.

It was Yves Saint Laurent who resurrected the jacket, with all its powerful messages. Yves said it himself: "Chanel freed women, I empowered them."[57] In the

Spring show of 1967, he introduced his unique version of the jacket, *le smoking*, (after the French word for tuxedo).

Using menswear fabrics, he softened the mannish silhouette with a smooth cut and a new take on men's tailoring. "He used traditional men's tailoring in a completely new way," according to one of the tailors who worked on the first *smokings*.[58] Adding to the striking new image of women, YSL paired these jackets with tailored trousers, and the pantsuit as we know it today was born.

The final touch, an example of Yves' supreme talent, were the accessories. These *les smokings* suits were worn with towering stiletto heels (a stunning innovation), dramatic jewelry, slinky transparent shirts. This was a costume forever removed from the mannish and Plain Jane outfits which had been favored by earnest social workers and Bohemian writers such as Gertrude Stein.

It was a deliciously androgynous and intensely alluring Look that is standard fare today. I mean, you can see a passable knockoff version right here in the 2003 Spiegel catalog — a nicely tailored double breasted jacket and sleek trousers in menswear pinstripe, worn with very high heels and dramatic earrings. (Women's and Misses sizes 4-16: $99.00)

We are so used to this uniform, seen on everyone from Gwyneth Paltrow to Hillary Clinton, it is difficult to imagine or recall that in 1967 a woman was banned from eating in the restaurant of the Plaza Hotel in Manhattan because she was wearing a YSL trouser suit. According to Parisian art director Maïmé Arnodin, *Elle* magazine wouldn't let their own writers and staff wear trousers to work, even though they were featuring article after article praising Yves and his *smokings*!

But we're talking about jackets here. The strong, androgynous style of Saint Laurent's vision, whether worn with trousers or a straight, fitted short skirt, was the definitive visual statement of the new expanded role that women intended to play on the world's stage. In the Eighties, the tailored jacket became the swat team uniform of women who Dressed for Success and who were aiming for that corner office.

The inevitable swing of the fashion pendulum brought another significant jacket symbol. Created by Italian designer Giorgio Armani, this jacket is a step back from strict menswear tailoring. His uniquely cut, soft, unstructured jackets are still expressions of power, but of power so absolute that it can whisper. His jackets are the uniform of dilettante heirs to great fortunes and relaxed billionaires — those who really don't have to try too hard or raise their voices because, with a languid wave of the hand, every order is carried out immediately by an eager underling. (And it had better be!)

You see Armani jackets on movie moguls, mega-movie stars (male and female), Saudi princes and the Mafia. The image carries with it something reminiscent of Eastern empires; Byzantium, Janissary assassins, the dark side of Venice — strange and sinister societies where power is so absolute that it can hide in softness — the better to disarm you.

Today, these are the three prototypes — classic Chanel, Saint Laurent's *le smoking* and Armani's sultanwear. Season after season, they're beautifully "interpreted" by the likes of Calvin Klein, Donna Karan and Ralph Lauren (who was once sued by Saint Laurent for — gasp! — copying. But never mind. The beat goes on.)

Whatever subtle meanings may cling to various interpretations of the jacket, the basic message, strong and powerful, is this. He/she who wears the jacket wears the mantle of authority. It's the magic garment idea, familiar in fairy tale and legend, and is part of the universal consciousness. The magic robe, cloak, or suit of armor invests the wearer with superhuman strength, wisdom, courage — or at least, a superhuman advantage, *i.e.* the cloak of invisibility of Harry Potter.

When a jacket talks, people listen. That was true yesterday, and it's true today. Jackets have the ability to confer power and authority and no single clothing symbol — other than a crown — does this more effectively. So, if that's what you want, a jacket will help you get it.

I can see that you're an extremely self-possessed woman who is seldom intimidated. Even so, a jacket can make your life easier. After all, *everyone* is faced, from time to time, with some situation that's demanding and potentially intimidating. Like what? Well, like returning things — *big* things — such as the Lexus you decided you don't want or those cruise tickets to Bora Bora. Wear a jacket and you'll probably get a full refund.

At a city council meeting, a jacket gives you the chutzpah to return those condescending "dear lady" responses with your own, "May I say to the *lovely* gentleman..." retorts. And at your children's school, when faced with a solid block of organized parental befuddlement, a jacket backs you up when you say, *"Screw the PTA!"*

So am I suggesting that you adopt that overdone, overly fashionable image that marks you as a member of the Ladies Who Lunch Club? Or the tired Dress for Success dictums of the long ago Eighties? Not at all.

Remember, it's the jacket itself that counts. It could be denim. (Naturally, not a faded, tattered version.) It could be red leather. It could be a biker jacket. (Now there's a style that gets results.) But it's the magic mantle of power, the jacket, that sends the symbolic message.

The world is yours in Black and a Jacket.

7

No

Wire

Hangers!!!

No Wire Hangers!!!

We're really being too hard on Joan Crawford. Sadly, revelations of her Medea-like motherhood have overshadowed the lustre of her screen presence. Though I must admit, in the definitive closet scene in her movie-biography *Mommie Dearest*,[59] Joan's diatribe about wire clothing hangers *does* seem a bit over wrought.

You remember the scene don't you? Crawford (played by Faye Dunaway) storms into her small daughter's room late one night. She flings open the closet doors and spies — Aha! — wire clothes hangers! Like a woman possessed, Joan sweeps the little, ruffled dresses onto the closet floor and raising a hanger to heaven in her clenched fist, screams the immortal lines: "No wire hangers! No wire hangers *ever*!!!"[60]

Yes, definitely over the top. But if we remember that for Joan, life had always been tough — whether in bleak orphanage dormitory or on velvet casting couch — perhaps we can be a bit charitable. Her hanger hysteria was not so much about caring for clothes as about living your dream. (Never mind that, according to daughter Christina, everyone else in her life was living a nightmare.)

There is still something to admire in Crawford's determination to *become* the screen goddess she portrayed and to live the fantasy she had created. At least that's the way I see it.

She must also have learned from superb costume designers like Adrian and Irene that lovely, costly garments need to be cherished and protected. She no doubt recognized that the essential line in any garment is the shoulder and sleeve line. It's the definitive perfecting contour in the same way that Joan's own cheekbones gave dramatic emphasis to her unforgettable face. Effective clothing maintenance means protecting that line. So of course, she would have recognized that wire hangers are totally inadequate to do the job.

Well, if not wire, what? The best clothing hangers are generously padded with fabric or are fashioned from sculptured wood. They can cost from ten to fifty dollars each. And they're worth it. But for those who are neither perfectionist nor princess, an ordinary plastic hanger (the freebie from the store) padded with tissue and secured with two rubber bands, works just fine.

By now, I guess you can tell. I subscribe to the Crawford Doctrine. I *hate* wire clothing hangers! But there's more to my wire hanger prejudice than their obvious functional inadequacy. I agree with Joan. They become a threat to any woman's dream of closet perfection and cause a sinister dumbing-down of any illusion one may have of maintaining high personal standards. What's even more insidious, wire hangers seem to proliferate in the unwary closet and then they Take Over. I caution you to avoid hanging two WCH's side by side in that darkened closet. Somehow they mate. Or amoeba-like, they split off into four, eight, sixteen units and become a clattering, chattering mob.

Obstinate and vexatious, they seem to have a life of their own, clinging to the closet bar when you are trying to disengage them, yet inexplicably sliding off the pole when you are nowhere near. And the way they treat your clothes! No matter how carefully one places blouse, jacket, dress or coat on a wire hanger, ten minutes later, half of these garments will be on the closet floor, abandoned and wretched, like the hapless wives of abusive husbands.

And while wire hangers *appear* to be made of wire, in use they take on Velcro™-like characteristics, catching on every possible surface. The hooked top becomes magically magnetic, with a special affinity for designer knits, chiffon, or fine lace, wreaking havoc on these delicate and expensive garments — Captain Hooks swashbuckling their way through your wardrobe.

Where do they come from, these wire wonders? Why, they come from the cleaners, of course. But wire clothing hangers are just one of the hazards that your clothes face when they have to go to — you know — the Big "C." (I think it's no coincidence that "being taken to the cleaners" is a synonym for personal loss and financial disaster.)

Whatever the state of your closet — whether mirrored elegance or institutional wallboard — wherever they hang, at some point, like a love affair gone wrong, your clothes will get dirty. They will have to leave their closet sanctuary and Go To The Cleaners.

Steady, now. Some important decisions need to be made. You must take on the attitude of a ruthless Beverly Hills hostess, look at your clothing companions and draw up your "A" list and your "B" list with cold-eyed pragmatism. Those clothes on the "A" list will go to the Truly Professional Cleaners, establishments which are capable of cleaning lilac suede jackets, wedding dresses, and possibly the royal robes of a newly discovered Egyptian mummy. Yes, they're good and they know it. Consequently, you may have to take out a loan on your car to pay the bill. It's kind of like sending your children to a very good prep school. Well worth it, if you can pay the tab.

The clothes on your "B" list, on the other hand, will be going to the dry cleaning version of an inner city school, a place where they will get little if any personal attention, will suffer from brutally overcrowded conditions and quite possibly, be the victims of violence. Some dry cleaners standards are so deplorable, we might create a new invective. "Go to Hell!" could become, "Oh, go to the Cleaners!"

Hang-Ups, The Secret Life of Clothes

Picture this. Acme Cleaners and Laundry — three o'clock on any afternoon. The meager air conditioning is no match for engulfing odors of caustic cleaning chemicals and the heavy, steam-laden air is pungent with the smell of singed and burning fabric. A swarthy man, heavyset and sweating profusely, is on the old-fashioned intercom.

"Hey, Sid. Yeah. It's me, Vinnie. What in the name of Holy Christ is going on down there?"

"I told ya'… there's trouble down the line. The Button Crusher's broken again."

"Shit! I thought your brother-in-law fixed it. Listen, we're stacked up here — dozens of shirts and silk blouses and sweaters, ready for The Starcher."

"Tell me about it. But you know the rules. Everything has to go through The Crusher."

And once you do retrieve your clothes, whether from Truly Professional haven or Acme hell, they face further challenges if you must put them back into your overburdened closet, where the clothes are packed-in like passengers on the 5 PM subway to Queens.

Obviously, the answer to keeping your clothes in excellent, ready-to-walk-out condition lies not only in the proper hanger and the nonviolent cleaner — you also need a functional closet. The challenges of the contemporary closet have not gone unnoticed by interior designers, efficiency experts, personal coaches and therapists of all kinds. ("I see that you're conflicted about this situation. Why not look at it this way? He's leaving you...but you'll have his closet.")

In the world of interior design, closets have become the new darling. The humble closet has moved miles beyond the "Go clean your room" dictums of childhood to become "multifunctional environments" as described on a recent Christopher Lowell TV show.[61]

As Lowell takes us on a tour of the Hancock Design House in Los Angeles, we are shown — ta-dah! — The Closet. This is a guest bedroom which has been transformed into the ultimate closet, with a design theme (Christopher tells us) of "40's style glamour" and "movie star indulgence." As the camera moves around the satined, mirrored, art-deco "environment," we don't need Christopher to tell us that this closet would make anyone feel like a Star. He goes on to describe the philosophy behind today's closets. They are expanded living spaces and may be furnished with chaises, love seats, lamps and tables, urns of flowers and entertainment areas.

On another TV show, Kathy Ireland, the star of HGTV's *Closets*, takes us to see several chic closets. "In 2002, this forgotten room has become the focal point of sophistication and style." In the home of "an international couple," we are shown that, "there's luxury everywhere. For example, the humble metal clothes poles have been sent out to be, not only lacquered, but antiqued as well…", the better to accommodate the delicate sensibilities of the custom sculptured cedar hangers. Price is no object in this multifunctional closet environment where, Ireland tells us, $9,000 dollars worth of lacquered teakwood enshrines the clothes. The designer explains, "You may be surprised to learn that this is *faux*-finish and not real teak." Yeah, with that price tag, we *are* surprised.

Our next stop is the Hawaiian home of a TV tycoon who has commissioned a closet of cathedral-like proportions and ambiance. It is 20 feet long with a vaulting ceiling that accommodates three levels of gleaming closets, wherein his Armani's and Karan's repose. It also features several oversized leather armchairs, a reading lamp, tables, flowers and perhaps — unknown to the public — a full kitchen!

If you are still struggling with the standard sliding door double closet, or even an overstuffed walk-in, possibly shared with That Man In Your Life ("All the space on this side of the red coat is MINE!"), these closet concepts have an aura of fantasy rivaling those daydreams of "If I won the lottery, I'd…"

It's not only TV that chronicles this new era of closet perfection. It's a favorite subject in magazines and books and fills colorful catalogs. Closet specialty stores are part of the mall scene, and closet design experts rival the personal trainer as an essential to The Good Life.

So, why this fascination with the ultimate closet? After all, closets themselves are a new footnote in the history of humankind. If you've visited the prehistoric cave dwellings in the south of France, you remember that there's nary a sliding door to be found. And even though the Bible tells us to, " go into your closet to pray…", I think that must have lost something in the translation, don't you? It didn't *really* mean your closet, even though some of the stuff in your current walk-in may appear to have been there since biblical times.

Actually, the architectural idea of a separate closet space is relatively new. In earlier times, most people didn't have enough clothes to need a closet, let alone two or three, as you no doubt do. True, royalty and their royal mistresses certainly needed closets. (There had to be a big payoff for bedding down with some of those royal losers — chunky Henry Vlll, for example.)

So there were wardrobe chambers, and Keepers of the Royal Robes. Even so, most of these clothes — dresses, robes, capes — were folded, sprinkled with herbs and *potpourri* and placed in wardrobe cupboards and chests. Or, in the case of his lordship's armor, in the *armoire*. The next time you're in a castle, look around. You'll see that there are no closets at all. But with the Industrial Revolution things changed, creating mass produced clothes and an emerging middle class to buy them. People needed more room for all their "stuff." Enter Closets!

The invention of closets had a profound effect on the theater, with closets playing a pivotal role which continues to this day. What would murder mysteries be without The Corpse in the Closet? And every spy or suspense drama needs its sinister Locked Closet. ("Oh, no, Mr. Bond. No one but Madame X has the key to *that* Closet.") But closets really come into their own in the bedroom farce, with a round robin of characters moving in and out of the bedroom closet like so many ponies on a carousel — the maid, the husband, the innkeeper, the chauffeur, etc. These scenes are terribly funny because, though exaggerated, they have the potential to mimic real life.

Whether in fact or fiction, today's expanded closet design brings an entirely new dimension to this familiar bedroom scene. We see a rumpled bed, two enthusiastic lovers. And then the woman suddenly raises her head. "Listen!" she whispers. *"Mon Dieu!* My husband has returned home. Quick! Hide in the closet...." Now, in the bad old days of conventional closets, the terrified lover would be forced to crouch, sweating and suffocating, in a crowded literal hole-in-the-wall (albeit with mirrored doors) until the all-clear.

In the current expanded setting, Mr. Macho strolls into the new, spacious "closet environment", mixes a drink, settles back into a leather armchair, and reads the sports page until the crisis has passed.

It becomes obvious that the purpose of today's closets is about much more than a place to store one's clothes. In today's world, what are closets expected to do? Closets — the new, ultra-organized, architecturally engineered, expanded closets — have become the status symbol of the new millennium, replacing the chef's kitchen of last season. You remember that one, don't you? The ubiquitous International Couple had their Aspen, St. Moritz, East Hampton's, kitchens remodeled to resemble the kitchens of Wolfgang Puck. (Never mind that they only use the microwave and that their trash bins reveal cartons and cartons of DiGiorno's.)

But the status closet has many more subtle payoffs than the status kitchen, which may be one more reason for its popularity. The status closet allows a woman to indulge in a delicious pastime, a favorite of the female of the species. This is a version of the male, "Mine's bigger than yours...", but is feminized to read, "Mine's more fashionable, more expensive, more elegant, more rarified. etc., than yours. And whatever it is, I have *more* of it." The status closet provides a woman with a convenient way to keep score, and suggests the need for a new version of the bumper sticker, "Whoever dies with the most toys wins" to read "Whoever dies with the *Most* wins!"

A recent article in *In Style* magazine[62] spells it out very clearly. Typical of the genre, this article pretends to be about storage and efficiency. But we're not fooled. We know how this game is played. The article is really about (1) *Things*; (2) These things are *mine*, All Mine; and (3)

"Don't you wish you were me?" (All the familiar themes from your freshman year in high school.)

Take the closet in designer Betsy Johnson's New York apartment. (And most of us would love to....) We are told that the spacious room — (*Room.* Did you catch that?) — is situated in the very center of her Fifth Avenue penthouse. "For Johnson, tidiness is the key." (Uh-huh!) "I'm very fine tuned and organized," the designer tells *In Style*.[63] Photographs show us her collections (*i.e.* Things.) stored in floor to ceiling shelves, everything in boxes that are neatly labeled — from Vivienne Woodward to vintage — and categorized. "I know every piece of junk I own," she tells *In Style* proudly. And when a collection of "junk" (Junk? Yeah, sure.) takes over a corner, she transports the excess to her remodeled red barn in upstate New York.

The section on designer Diane Von Furstenberg tells us that the designer has a love-hate relationship with her shoes. "One moment she adores each and every loafer, stiletto and pump in the *shoe closet*." (Emphasis added because I'm ready to kill myself!) Then, we are told, she takes a sweeping look at the more than 400 pairs before her and cries, "It's obnoxious! It's ghastly!" (It's *mine!*)

Photographs in her West Village carriage house show us that the cavernous lime-green shoe closet is a picture of order and discipline with the shoes organized according to season and style; dressy shoes in one section, winter boots in another, fabrics and leathers (alligator, snakeskin, suede, satin, denim, etc.) in yet another. "I keep my shoes until they fall apart," Von Furstenberg tells us. "I have more shoes at my home in Connecticut." And does she have any favorites? A pair of custom made boots by Louboutin are her current infatuation. "But shoes are like men. The one of the moment is the favorite." Right, Diane. So many shoes. So little time.

Natalie Cole's twin closets "...hold enough clothes to impress till the next Ice Age," *In Style* reports. "And they also house her sixty seven pairs of sunglasses, each in their proper designer case." Three other closets handle the overflow. "Maybe I should add another wing,"[64] she worries. Don't fret, Natalie! You'll work your way through this.

In the foregoing sarcastic review of closet overkill, you've no doubt picked up my hidden agenda. It really doesn't take the psychiatric version of a rocket scientist to figure this one out. I ridicule what I desire. It's true. I, too, want The Perfect Closet. *I want it!* I want the oversized, extravagant, disgustingly excessive closet that I've been describing.

I see it now. A huge room, with shelves reaching from floor to very high ceiling, each shelf divided into perfectly proportioned sections and in each section a perfectly fitting clear plastic box. No, wait! Not plastic. Am I crazy? Each box is covered with faille — peach-colored, I think — with a little card on the front to tell what's in the box. No. Erase that. The boxes are numbered — *in polished brass. And there's an oversized book covered in faille that's a sort of directory. No, wait! Maybe the whole system is automated and all my clothes are on a moving conveyor belt like the one they have at the cleaners....*

But it is all too much for me. Maybe I'll just buy some of those plastic boxes at Target. And I'll get rid of some of this stuff. I'll put the overflow in my U-Store Closets cubicle. Maybe I'll do that next week.

The truth is, most writers (even fashion chroniclers) live a life with definite Miss Haversham overtones. It is a life that makes closet perfection almost impossible, since we never throw any piece of paper away. An obscure word, a phrase, a quirky bit of information, an article from *American Heritage, Scientific American,* or *The Enquirer* — any and all may be useful sometime in that patchwork quilt of facts and ideas, transposed to sentences, paragraphs and chapters that will be "that next book." Then all of these bits are catalogued and filed and stored in boxes. And boxes. These boxes hide under elegant table skirts, behind dining room doors, on the tippy-top shelves in the kitchen. And of course, in closets.

Still, I'll continue to fantasize about the perfect closet. And if you don't already possess one, I'll bet you will, too. Because closets have an even deeper appeal than the ego-driven motives we've been discussing. The perfect closet doesn't just symbolize affluence and luxury — which are certainly appealing. But over and above that, the perfect closet holds out the promise of a perfectly ordered life, with you in control.

Moreover, it is transformational. With the perfect closet comes the perfect You. While you may not have the penthouse or the chic-ly remodeled red barn, with the perfect closet you could become that perfect, "Don't you wish you were me?" woman. As actress Felicity Huffman confided about her closet aspirations: "One day, I should like to be a woman who uses shoe trees." And I think we all can get a sense of what she means.

In fact, the closet is such a meaningful symbol to us, it is often used as a metaphor for a woman's life. This closet symbol is a segue and an update from a universal theme in woman's psychic history which is, "I am my house." We could look to many fairy tales for examples — Snow White, safe from all sexual competition in the snug little dwarves' house. Or Sleeping Beauty, whose sexuality is locked away and slumbering in the thorn protected castle. Or Beauty and the Beast, wherein Beauty lives in all the luxury that a castle can provide. The only price is that she learn to love the Beast. (And can we find real life counterparts to this little fable? Hey! Let's not even go there!)

But for the most dramatic and instructive symbolism, as usual we can count on Hollywood. In her excellent book, *A Woman's View: How Hollywood Spoke to Women, 1930-1960*, author Jeanine Basinger delineates this "I am my house" concept as one of the dominant themes in women's movies. In these films, Basinger writes that the house "…represents who the woman is, both as a physical representation of her inner turmoils and a reflection of where she stands on the social scale." In the 30s, 40s and 50s, "it is the space the woman is allowed, her place to dominate."[65]

The house is so important a space in the woman's film world that it is actually a character in several films of the Forties; *Enchantment* (1948), *The Enchanted Cottage* (1945), and *Secret Beyond the Door* (1948)[66]. However, proof that the house is still an eloquent metaphor is seen in a more recent movie.

Fast-forward to 2002. In *Crossroads*,[67] starring Britney Spear, her mother's house tells us everything we need to know about the pivotal event in the life of Lucy, Britney's movie character. What were the reasons the mother chose to abandon her husband and three year old daughter? That is the core question of our heroine's life. As the story unfolds, Lucy arranges to see her mother again. It will be the first meeting of mother and daughter in 15 years. Lucy's friends drive her up to her mother's house and we immediately learn a lot about the mother's character as we view her house — an imposing hacienda style with a manicured cactus garden, surrounded by a high stuccoed wall.

Our heroine's reception is definitely chilly — not at all what the girl had anticipated. Her mother, the perfect image of polished, upscale matron, reluctantly invites Britney into the coldly perfect living room. The furniture is formal, stiff, controlled. The mother compulsively straightens an already perfect sofa pillow, removes an invisible speck from a table. It's clear. She doesn't want this unexpected, inconvenient daughter to ruffle the surface of her perfectly ordered life. And so she rejects her own child. But we're not surprised. The house told us everything.

If the house represents the woman's social self and her place in society, then the closet symbolizes her inner life — with all its secrets.

In Hitchcock's *Rebecca*[68] (1940), the mansion Manderley "...represents not only the dreaded first wife of Lawrence Olivier, but also the evil she brought into his life,"[69] says Basinger. This movie also has one of the definitive movie closet scenes, a scene that clearly illustrates the essence of the closet metaphor. In this scene, Rebecca's closet is used as a symbol of her evil sexuality — a power that she has used to exploit everyone in her life.

Manderley's housekeeper, the sinister Mrs. Danvers, has enticed the shy second wife to view the bedroom of Rebecca, a room which has been closed since her untimely death. Mrs. Danvers, who seems to have a disturbingly intense attachment to Rebecca, propels the reluctant young woman to the dressing room and Rebecca's closet. "You'd like to see her clothes, wouldn't you?" she whispers to the terrified girl (who, in Mrs. Danvers' words, "will never take Rebecca's place.")

There are distinct lesbian undertones to the scene as the housekeeper reveals the intriguing contents of Rebecca's closet. Slowly opening the mirrored doors, caressing each spectacular garment as she removes it, Danvers proffers each silk, each velvet, each fur for the young wife to see, touch and smell. These are the exquisite things that enfolded Rebecca's loveliness.

Like a swan with a cobra, the younger woman is mesmerized by the power of Rebecca's closet presence. The evil housekeeper propels her to the window and whispers, "He never loved you. You can never take Rebecca's place… why don't you just let it all go…" Does the young wife leap out into the swirling fog and leave Manderley to the triumphant Rebecca? It's a terrific movie. Rent it and find out!

In *American Gigolo* (1980)[70], it's a man whose closet is his sexual alter-ego. In this movie, Richard Gere (in his delicious prime) is living a life we usually associate with women, *i.e.* trading sexual favors for money. So we might project that he has feminized his relationship with his closet. (And yes, I know that prostitution is not limited to the female of the species and that there are a zillion male prostitutes out there. But we're talking symbolism here. And male hustlers, no doubt unfairly, are usually not associated with sleek, call-girl glam. And that's what Gere is in this movie…a gorgeous call-boy.)

So, in the closet scene, Gere is getting ready for a client "appointment." He mixes a drink, lights up a joint, and feeling ever-so-mellow, starts preparations for his work — an encounter with yet another love starved middle-aged woman. It is time to present his sexual publicity. He opens the double doors of a large closet and we see a dazzling array of Armani's, Brioni's and Kiton's. There is enough Italian silk to clothe the Mafia worldwide.

He stands and admires his treasures, then pulls out several jackets and slacks and throws them on the bed. He slides open a silent drawer to reveal dozens of shirts, also silk, also rich and elegant in the muted colors only the best quality can produce. He again makes several choices, places them on the bed, and goes through a similar ritual with the ties. Then he languidly plays with the clothing combinations. Should he wear this one or that, combine this color with that one, etc. He really is having a love affair with his clothes, the trophies that make his life style not just bearable, but richly fulfilling. They are the badges of success and adoration from satisfied (Boy! Are they satisfied...) clients.

In *Breakfast at Tiffany's* (1960)[71] — the quintessential Audrey Hepburn movie — we see yet another revealing closet scene. At one point, we catch a glimpse of the inside of Holly Golightly's closet. It is starkly minimal. There are just three or four garments hanging there; a trench coat, a black dress, a fashionable orange coat. On the shelf, a perfect black hat. This minimalism represents her determination to erase her past (which, as the plot unfolds, we see was terribly lower class and messy, worlds away from the present life of this breezy, sophisticated party girl.) In effect, Holly (Audrey Hepburn) is determined to let nothing into her closet — and no one into her life — that doesn't conform to her ideal of the new life she *will* live.

And this becomes the main conflict as the love story unfolds. She rejects George Peppard. (So adorable in this movie…how could she?) He represents real life and true love. But she is torn, and with ruthless determination chooses the fantasy lover, the weak and shallow Argentine millionaire. Does true love triumph, ultimately? Of course you remember how it ends.

Another universal theme inherent in the idea of closets is a woman's need for *things*: houses, china, clothes, jewelry (sunglasses!). "I want things!" is the anguished cry of actress Peggy Cummins in *Gun Crazy* (1949)[72]. As author Basinger tells us, "She utters the battle cry of movie females, 'I want things…*big* things!'"[73] In or out of the movies, this line resonates like a bell.

You may say, "Why, most of these examples are from the past. Woman have moved far, far beyond such pitiful aspirations. After all, women have taken an evolutionary leap from drudge to doctor, from lowly housewife to lawyer and CEO. Things! How shallow. How mundane." And how elemental. Stocks and bonds are fine. Crashing through that glass ceiling to the corner office is satisfying.

But it is alien territory. The Goddess calls. On some visceral level, every woman wants things — lots of exquisite things. And a fabulous place to keep them.

This is the genius of Martha Stewart. She's tapped into this omnipresent craving and millions of women resonate to her insightful message. The trophies for a successful woman (as we've already seen) are not the male symbols of success — fast cars and loose women. No, a woman wants *things*. And a fantasy closet!

This desire for Her Things is part of woman's ancient history. One thinks of East Indian women wearing their dowries of elaborate gold jewelry, of Hope Chests and Trousseau Trunks, of the rich caravans that carried biblical daughters to their nuptials, protected and empowered by their personal treasure.

Yes, things are dependable. Beauty fades, men leave, children disappoint. But you can count on things. It's the timeless wisdom of Lorelei Lee, "Diamond's Are A Girl's Best Friend."[74] The marvelous difference between then and now is this: you want things? You can get them all by yourself!

The next time you are in a reflective mood, reviewing your life, perhaps adding up the score, you may feel that finally, in your own estimation, you have *arrived!* If, however, you are not quite sure, if you have doubts about your life's accomplishments and the unfolding of your personal drama up to this point, you can look to your closet. It will provide you with a TV Guide synopsis of Your Life Thus Far.

Have you always been pampered and treasured, the Jewish Princess syndrome in the truest sense of the word? That is, the jewel of the family — and like all jewels, in its perfect setting. Then I have no doubt at all that you have a closet (or more likely, closets) that are the envy of every girlfriend — and even your critical mother-in-law. Your closets will be an extension of life as it has always been for you, with *you* as the center. It is the natural order of things.

Ah, but what if your life has been somewhat different? If the story of you and your siblings was, "Mother always liked *you* best"…or if that early atmosphere was Spartan and you were a victim of benign neglect (or worse)…if you have survived dangerous men and foolish choices…or if you have endured dutiful sacrifices — then, my friend, indulge yourself with a luxurious closet.

Get out your credit cards and the *Hold Everything* catalog and Go For It! Create that nurturing, acknowledging, inspiring altar to one's Self that is The Perfect Closet.

(And for heaven's sake, throw out those wire hangers!!!)

8

Closing
the Closet

Closing the Closet

$\mathcal{S}$omehow, I never imagined I'd have much in common with comedian George Burns. I don't smoke cigars. I tell jokes badly. And _I_ can sing. But in a TV interview many years after the death of his beloved Gracie, George confided a very personal and touching story that has remained with me, and ultimately has become a meaningful part of my life.

He told about disposing of Gracie's clothes after she passed away, explaining that he and their daughter gave to friends and family the beautiful clothes that Gracie had loved so much. But one dress — a favorite of hers — George kept. He went on to explain that this dress "lived" in his closet thereafter. Hanging beside his jackets and slacks, it created for him an ongoing presence of Gracie, the wife he so obviously adored.

Last Christmas, when I was completing the dispersal of my mother's things, I remembered George Burns. It had been a year since my mother passed away, but I was still involved in the seemingly endless tasks that accompany the death of a loved one. (You probably can relate to this — if not now, you will.) For example, it seems so outrageous that you still have to deal with the income taxes of the deceased — long after they have moved to that care-free tax haven in the sky! This and other mundane obligations seemed so utterly oppressive and unfair. But at last, I was coming to the end of the list.

So here I was, a few days before Christmas, pulling in to a parking place near the local Battered Woman's Center. I was there because I had responded to an appeal for warm coats "at this season when everyone's heart should open to the need..." I had dispensed with all of my mother's clothes at this point, except for one item, a jaunty car coat that had been one of her last purchases. It was the result of a fun shopping trip with her, an afternoon when she seemed to be her old self, a delightful and amusing companion — and a formidable fashion expert. What could be a more deserving fate for this favorite garment?

I got the coat out of the back of the car and started down the block to the Center's entrance, carrying that soft, warm quilted coat, its *faux* fur collar still pristine and elegant. But my steps faltered, and then stopped. In spite of my detached resolve, somehow, I just couldn't move ahead. Perhaps the need for warm coats wasn't *that* great. (After all, this was California.) Maybe I could just forget the whole thing.

I turned and started back to the car. Then my intellectual self reminded me of the worthiness of this cause, my need to "get organized and move on" and finally, a sarcastic jab, "Don't be ridiculous!" I started back to the Center with a firm step and a firmer grip on the coat. But I paused again, and took a couple of steps back towards the car. Finally, I stopped dead — right in the middle of the sidewalk. And gave up.

It was the George and Gracie, dress -in-the -closet story all over again. That car coat is now hanging in my own closet, ensconced with my other coats in a too crowded space. I'll never wear it and I don't need it. But of course, that's not true. I *do* need it. It's just nice to know it's there.

It seems clear. Clothes retain the essence of the wearer's personality, just as a good perfume will infuse a dress or sweater with a reminder of the scent. Years after the garment has been put away in a trunk, forgotten, when you open that trunk and unwrap the tissue paper, a subtle aroma of the original perfume remains.

In the same way, when people we love die, it is often their clothes that keep them close with an ineffable presence. And in retrospect, the clothes that women choose — especially those beloved treasures, those favorite companions, those PR agents that tell the world their story — these clothes (or the recollection of them) can bring forth the most moving memories.

Can you remember any of the clothes your mother wore when you were a little girl? If you can remember, it's such sweet nostalgia to think back to a time in your childhood when your mother was dressed for some special occasion. Suddenly, she seemed to be a totally different and lighthearted person, transformed from the responsible Guardian of All Things, including the consumption of green vegetables.

Or perhaps you remember her in her "uniform," the daily wardrobe statement you recall from childhood. Incidentally, these memories don't need to be post-mortems. You could be looking across a lunch table at your mother next week, and remembering what she wore to your ballet classes. It could be a revealing and evocative memory, re-creating a happy scene that may smooth the bumps in the road as crotchety age approaches. (Hers, not yours!)

I can remember most of my mother's clothes in the most scrupulous detail, especially at that period of my childhood when I was about five or six. My father, an army officer, was stationed at Fort Warden near the little town of Port Townsend in Washington State. At that time, the Army, like everything else in American life, was much more formal and structured. For the officers, there were many receptions and cocktail parties and dinners. In addition, as part of the Army's community relations, officers were sent to city and charity functions to represent the military's presence in the local community and in Seattle. Because my parents were attractive and charming, they were often asked to be the Army's representatives at these affairs.

So my mother needed clothes — lots of pretty and suitable outfits —suits, dresses, hats, gloves, purses. She bore up under this responsibility with admirable grace.

Her favorite shop was the Elaine Craig Shoppe (yes, with an "*e*"). Far from the sophistication of Seattle, this was a bastion of fashion and elegance in northwestern Washington. At the change of every fashion season, Miss Craig would travel to New York to shop and order. Then, she'd return to the hinterlands of Port Townsend and call her special customers. Mother was an obvious favorite, not only because of the size of her purchases, but because she had such flair.

After one of these phone calls, I could anticipate a magical afternoon with my mother, who would return home from the *shoppe* with a collection of bags and boxes all a-rustle with tissue paper. We would go into her bedroom, unwrap *everything* and put the treasures out on the bed, organizing and completely accessorizing all the outfits until they resembled a group of snoozing mannequins, awaiting their call to the runway.

I can remember so many of these costumes in the most minute detail. It amazes me. For example: there was a navy gabardine coat that flared out from the shoulders via a series of bias cut panels. It had full sleeves with buttoned cuffs, creating a sort of Gallic painter's smock feeling. With it, she had chosen a navy straw beret in the softest weave ever. I remember because we crushed it this way and that to see how it would look the most flattering.

The companion to this coat was a red silk dress in a small navy and white print, very slim, with a draped neckline. And then there was the grey wool fitted coat and matching skirt, with a textured stripe woven into the pearl grey fabric. The blouse that accompanied this coat-suit was navy silk taffeta overlaid with a plaid print in silvery threads. It sported a big, pussycat bow at the neckline. (We decided that the beret looked perfect with this outfit, too.)

Another costume was a tawny gold knit dress with a brown suede belt and an ornate brass buckle. The hat? Let's see…. Yes. It was a paisley turban. My mother looked *great* in turbans. Whenever she wore a turban, people told her she looked like Dorothy Lamour. Which irritated her mightily, for some reason.

Of course there were evening dresses too, remembered in a different context, in a flurry and rush of last minute directions to the baby sitter while my father stood impatiently at the door. "Come *on*, Minn."

One evening in particular — how can I remember it so clearly? My father seems so tall to my six year old eyes, so strong and wonderful. And my mother! She is wearing a black crepe evening dress that has a striking halter neckline and low-cut back. Thinking about that dress now, I realize that it was dramatic, slinky, daring. It was dynamite! This for a woman who never, to my knowledge, allowed the word sex to pass her lips. Funny, isn't it. You never *really* know your parents.

She is standing in the hall now, looking at herself in the mirror. My father is looking at her, too, and smiling.

"Wait! It needs something." she says, and hurries back into their bedroom. She comes out waving a large, red chiffon handkerchief. I know it well. It is embroidered with gold *fleur-de-lis* and is, for me, a rainy day treat. I have been allowed, on occasion, to use it in dress-up adventures. She flares it out in a grand *chiffon* gesture, then tucks the corner of the kerchief into the jeweled belt of her gown. "There!" She's right. It's perfect.

Fast forward many years. My mother and I have switched roles. We are like those Swiss clocks where figures move in and out of the lime light, depending on the hour. The time has come for me to be center stage. I am now the tall one, the strong one, the sole support in illness and crisis. As my mother travels along the predictable road of extreme old age, I see myself as her coach, trying to help her meet her next great adventure in whatever way I am able. But it is not easy, as you yourself may know. After all, she is on a road that I have yet to travel.

It is sad and challenging and one must keep reminding oneself to be compassionate, that it takes great courage to grow very old. In this atmosphere, I am constantly looking for diversions and amusements and *passatempo* occasions, something, *anything*, to brighten her mood and to lift her out of a prevailing melancholy.

When I read of the Halloween dance at our local senior center, I thought this would be such an opportunity. (She and my father had loved to dance. They were excellent dancers too, and I could remember being delighted and a little scandalized — with the prudishness of child-hood —when they would occasionally dance around the living room. Then, too, my mother loved music and played the piano very well. A real ragtime gal, she pounded out rollicking renditions of *Kitten on the Keys* and *St. Louis Blues.*)

Maybe this dance would be fun! Her response was an enthusiastic, "Let's go!" And so, here we are at the Halloween Ball. It's fortunate that there is an oversized sparkling banner proclaiming the event, because otherwise, the bare public hall with its gaggle of folding chairs bears little resemblance to a gala party.

What I see instead are two long, paper covered tables set out with cookies and Kool-Aid™, some balloons and streamers. a *papier mache* jack-o-lantern. The hosts are *trying!* In a further kind attempt by the sponsors to make this a party, they have engaged live music for the evening. The trio — a piano player, a guitarist, and a drummer — are, we are informed by an ornate sequined sign, The Dreamboats.

The piano player is the quintessential piano teacher from our childhood. Steel rimmed glasses emphasize her severely earnest expression as she leans forward to peer at the sheet music propped up on the piano stand. (One looks for a gold star in the margin of the music and a clicking metronome to complete the picture.)

The guitar player is one of those red, white and blue ladies, wearing the colorful and brave uniform that is a favorite target of slick young comediennes — blue hair, white powdered complexion, and a Revlon-red slash of color where lips used to be.

But it is the drummer who is the true star of the evening. He plays his instrument with an overpowering beat that reverberates throughout the hall. It becomes a radar vibration that dancers with deaf ears can *feel*. They can "get with the beat" even though they can no longer hear *Everybody Loves My Baby* or *Puttin' on the Ritz*.

It's strange. Even though the drummer is a very old man (his shirt collar is as big as a Christmas wreath around his wasted neck), you can still see the shy, gangling youth, practicing his drums in a drafty garage ("Get that damned noise out of here…"), dreaming his Big Band dreams.

Tah-dah-dah. *Tah*-dah-dah. Round and round, like a carousel of grotesques in a Fellini film, the dancers move with uneven steps.

One old man, pale and faltering, is dressed in a devil's costume. His long face, under the horned headdress, looks not at all like Satan but more like that of a tired sheep. His lady, in a tall pointed witch's hat and black gauzy robe, is much too close to the fairy tale prototype of a cackling old crone to make this a wise costume choice. She, too, is very solemn, looking past her partner, lips moving as she counts out the time to the music. Two old ladies in vague harem costumes, beyond any possibility of male companionship, dance together wordlessly, with an occasional tussle to determine who is leading.

The scene is so overwhelming in its contrasts — all the gaiety, romance, and lighthearted fun that are implicit in the words "Halloween Ball", the banner, the balloons, the streamers, the promise of fun and escape. And this reality of faded dreams, sad endings, and the valor of these dear old souls going through the motions. I can barely control the wave of emotion that threatens to become an audible cry. And then, there comes the guilty realization that it is I who have engineered this terrible experience for my mother.

Do I dare look at her? Can I bear to share this scene with her? Over a lifetime of shared joys, crises and various dramas, we so often have been on the same wavelength. But "What is shared is more easily born" and so, as much for her sake as for mine, I do look at her, expecting to see a reflection of my own despairing mood.

But she doesn't appear to be sad or depressed. In fact, her face is more animated and lively than it has been for a very long time. Her eyes are bright and a small smile warms and softens her face. She is tapping her foot —*Tah*-dah-dah — in time to the music as she watches the dancers faltering round and round the dance floor.

Hang-Ups, The Secret Life of Clothes

And then I realize that she isn't seeing these aged dancers in their improbable costumes. She isn't seeing them at all. She is seeing, instead, a handsome, adoring man in an officer's uniform, a slender young woman in a black crepe evening dress. And a handkerchief of red chiffon.

9

What Do Women Want?

What Do Women Want?

*W*hat do women want? That was Freud's petulant question, repeated often in his writings. What, indeed? It's an age old riddle and perplexed men have been seeking the answer since they were chucked out of Eden. What do women want? Freud, *et al*, didn't know.

But I do. We want a lot of simple and obvious things that we're not getting. Like what?

Like department store dressing rooms "bigger than a bread box", with flattering — no, we'd settle for tolerable — light.

> *For God's sake, Macy's, Bloomie's and Sak's! Give us lighting that's not been imported from some subterranean CIA interrogation room. Help us a little with our illusions. It is* you, *with your merciless fluorescent lighting, who are responsible for making The Day I Buy A Bathing Suit the Worst Day of the Year.*

Here's another Freudian question. Why does a woman need a fly?

In a world awash with Ab-Blasters, Torso Tamers, Belly Busters, and countless other devices designed to trim those extra inches from the front of our bodies, why do we women need that extra three quarters of an inch of bulky fabric, zipper or buttons across our bellies?

Granted, fashion mag photos of sixteen year old models, their fly's provocatively open by two or three unengaged buttons, are definitely arresting. But most of us keep our pants buttoned — at least in public. With maturity, we recognize that the unbuttoned fly may get you arrested.

I think the message about sun glasses is getting through. No more sly, reptilian little "druggie" glasses. They're so Jack Nicholson. We want — need — BIG celebrity sunglasses. (I know. They're definitely Jackie-O. Is that bad?) The kind of glasses with Presence. The kind that make a woman look as if she is The Great and Good Friend of some incredibly powerful man.

One of the most useful bits of fashion advice I've ever gotten came from an international friend of mine who travels the world and knows what's what.

At one time, I had confided to her that I was seriously contemplating a move to Mexico City (for a variety of interesting reasons which I'll write about one day). I shared with her my concern about functioning comfortably and effectively, as a woman living alone in that macho Latin society.

She told me that I'd be just fine if I followed her advice: have plenty of attitude, wear lots of black, all my jewelry, and (very important) large intimidating Power Sunglasses. The implication? "I am the pampered darling of someone very influential. And I'm taking names!"

What else do women want? A solution to the stocking thing. Currently, many women are saying, "The hell with it!" And the moment the temperature gets above freezing, well, they simply go without. But please. Be merciful. Lots and lots of calves out there — pale, veined, too thin or too fat — can definitely use the magic wands of Nylon™ and Lycra™. Still, I can absolutely empathize with this libertarian attitude, because pantyhose are a daily challenge.

> Certainly, no man should ever be allowed to watch the woman in his life putting on a pair of control top pantyhose. The writhing, the twisting, the grunting, the heavy breathing. And the final indignity — shoving that extra three pounds of avoirdupois into its Lycra™ prison.

> Then — gasp! — pulling up, up, UP on the panty-section. In spite of my description and the heavy breathing part ("What are you wearing right now?") this routine just doesn't have the same mystique as pulling on a pair of very tight jeans.

Or, there's the other extreme.

> Carefully, carefully rolling each silken stocking leg up the calf and thigh, a ritual performance worthy of an acolyte to some strange cult, smoothing and guiding the fabric — and then, merde! And an outburst of truck driver profanity that

no man should hear from his Love bursts forth as we lament the fatal "run." The coup de grâce *has been administered by a rough finger nail or an unsuspected chair rung.*

No wonder women in movies always wear garter belts and stockings. Or nothing at all.

And speaking of movies, just where are all the Great Movie Clothes? We want to see fabulous clothes IN the movies, not just on the <u>way</u> to the movies — as Red Carpet interviewers analyze the borrowed finery draped on various stars, starlets and industry hangers-on.

It's interesting that interviews with some of Hollywood's newest young stars reveals a fascination and Gee Whiz devotion to the movies of fashion icons Grace Kelly and Audrey Hepburn. Even at this distance, to be enveloped in the beauty and magic of their movies is an enchanting experience — an almost mystical journey into an elemental aspect of the female essence.

Kelly's Rear Window,[75] To Catch a Thief[76], The Swan[77]. *And Hepburn's* Funny Face[78], Sabrina[79], Two For The Road[80]. *These movies delivered. Who can forget the quintessential Audrey in her Breakfast at Tiffany's black dress* cum *pearls and cheese Danish?*

But today's movies? There's no magic there.

Fast forward to Julia Roberts in *Notting Hill*[81]. If you recall, in this romantic comedy Roberts is portraying a mega-movie star. We, the audience, are being primed in the opening scenes with the message that she is the world's sweetheart. We can hardly wait for our first sight of this fabulous Being. So, when we do see Julia in Hugh Grant's little book store, what is the world's sweetheart wearing? Shapeless, ordinary, athletic clothes, a scarf twisted any old way over her hair, and huge, black clodhopper shoes.

OK. The director wanted to convey a mood, an incognito laid-back image. I get it. But an inspired director teamed with a costume designing artist would create that same mood — but in a costume with so much flair and pizzaz — every woman in the audience would want it, too.

I'll give you another example. A couple of years ago, when Pierce Brosnan was announced as the new James Bond, everyone eagerly awaited the fantasy and the wonderful excesses of the Bond tradition. And the arrival of a new "Bond Girl." In past movies, these ladies had been extraordinary creatures — gorgeous, alluring, dangerous — in outrageous costumes. Great fun.

But when the new Bond Girl appeared, what a letdown! She kick-boxed her way to Brosnan's side in a sweat suit and running shoes. I know. That's very Now. But she was as bland as her outfit, which was as ordinary as anything you could buy at Target. No, I take that back. They have cute things at Target. So why not design for Ms. Bond Girl the most fabulous sweat suit you ever imagined? The kind of thing that would get us right up out of our seats and To The Malls, where the studio-licensed knockoffs would be waiting.

Maybe they'll get the message for the next Bond adventure. We'll see.

What else do women want? Some women dream of a phantom lover in the closet — ever ready to smooth their feelings, to flatter them and make them feel wonderful about the way they look. My fantasy is different. I want an ironing board in the closet, which would provide many of the same benefits. In my walk-in closet (or closet *room* as we've already discussed), the ironing board would be in it's own little cupboard, always there, sturdy, dependable, eager for a pressing "quicky".

Instead. many of us are contending with these collapsible, fold-up boards that are quirky and unpredictable. Putting them up is like trying to dance the tango with an unwilling partner. (Don't any of these manufacturers have fingernails?)

Take my advice. If you are building a new house, or remodeling, do not neglect to tell your architect that what women want is a closet ironing board. This is a <u>must</u> and will do wonders for your disposition — just like a secret lover.

This is just a personal thing, but I'd like to see more people overdressed. Not casual, not understated. But rather with a little too much of everything. You know, really Put Together — wearing dramatic clothes, imaginative accessories that make a statement, important makeup and hair, lots of jewelry. Stuff that's fun to look at.

(Maybe I'm not spending enough time in Texas.)

Salespeople: O.K. Call me crazy. Call me cranky. Call me politically incorrect. While I'd be the first to admit that accents can be charming — it's so pleasant, so efficient when your salesperson at the very least, *understands* English.

Speaking of being cranky, there's nothing like sore feet to make a woman lose her charm and charisma. I think I speak for women everywhere when I say, "I'd love to see a return to shoes that fit. I mean, that fit *me*."

I used to wear a very narrow-sized shoe. A Quad, it used to be known as. When I was growing up, my mother made a big thing out of being sure that my shoes fit properly. There was always lots of, " Walk around on the carpet and see if they really support your arch…" kind of talk.

And there were serious consultations with the clerk, who typically assumed the demeanor of a top orthopedic specialist from Vienna. To enhance this image, clerks were often supplied with an elaborate device for measuring your foot. You had to stand up, fit your foot just so and press down hard, onto the calibrated contraption.

But in recent years, it has become harder and harder to find narrow shoes. First the AAAA width disappeared. Then the Triple-A. A few years ago, the Double was gone, too. Almost all shoes today, except for the most expensive, seem to come in the ubiquitous Medium.

Still, there is a fortunate result to all these improperly fitting shoes. Year by year, my unsupported feet have grown wider. I figure if I just live long enough, I may finally fit in!

Now, about boots. Every Autumn, when the exciting new winter fashions appear, the word from the top is, "Boots! Boots with everything." That makes total fashion sense, since boots visually elongate the leg, add drama to any outfit, and make you look mah-velous. Consequently, almost every woman loves boots. We're already sold. *Vogue, Elle, Bazaar, et al* go on to instruct us, "Boots complete The Look. They're warm. They're wonderful. They're wearable."

Wait. Stop right there. They are <u>not</u> wearable.

For the last four or five years, the boots that appear in every store, shop, or boutique, have heels the height of the Empire State building. Many of these boots are so weird looking, they would delight the hearts of any fetishist or purveyor of The Oldest Profession.

Some of these boots not only have sky scraper heels but half inch platforms, too. Yes, we know who wears these kinds of boots. But frankly, few of us want to whip through the daily events of our lives dressed like a dominatrix. (Though it might come in handy in billing controversies with plumbers and mechanics.)

And if this sounds like the grumpy grousing of an aging Boomer, let me remind you that the top models in the world — ages seventeen to twenty two — regularly fall off their sky high shoes on the runways of Paris.

So please. What women want are good looking, great fitting, wearable boots — with 3" heels, tops.

Here's a message for Wall Street and Seventh Avenue. When it comes to new looks, new styles, new directions for clothes and shoes and jewelry and wonderful fashion — what do women want? What do I want?

I don't know! (OK. So I lied when I said I knew all the answers.)

It's up to <u>you</u>, the design geniuses, the fashion czars, the retail emperors, to figure it out. It's time for you to stop kvetching about the vanishing bottom line and to come up with irresistible, thrilling, I-can't-live-without-it, kinds of clothes.

Of course, one can drop in to Chanel or Gucci and find just such delicious fashions. But what about the real world, the affordable world of Macy's and Nordstrom, Ann Taylor, Banana Republic and the ever-present Gap? Across the board, the retail industry is in trouble.

The president of the Gap was recently interviewed and asked to comment on the most recent of a series of dismal profit showings. He said, in effect, "We got away from our true image. We're returning to the wonderful Gap basics."

Ho-hum. You mean the same bland basics that we can buy at Old Navy, Mervyn's, T.J. Maxx, etc.? Same quality. For a lower price.

Listen. All you company presidents should go to Paris. Not to the Collections, but to some of the wonderful mass retail shops that are part of that real world. Just two examples are Carroll, a chain of retail shops, much like the American chains I've mentioned, or Redoute (who also offer a catalog). These stores feature The Basics, too. But they are basics with a visible plus. *La difference* is — the style, the flare, the fit, the imaginative cut.

These clothes, just like those from U.S. based companies, are made in Korea or Thailand or — well, you know the places. But somehow, the French get it right. They create such delightful and irresistible clothes, you don't care if your credit cards are maxxed. *You've just gotta have it!*

What else do women want?

Real men.

Bras that fit.

Lo-fat ice cream that's truly delicious.

Blusher that stays on for more than an hour.

And, let's see...

I'm still working on my list. I'll get back to you.

Appendices

Footnotes

1. See Filmography. (A runner-up to this all-time old-robe movie is *When Harry Met Sally.*)

2. See Filmography

3. Refers to characters in *Pygmalion*, a play by George Bernard Shaw. It was later made into the movie *My Fair Lady*. See Filmography.

4. See Filmography.

5. See Filmography.

6. See Filmography.

7. *Ninotchka.* Garbo's first comedy. See Filmography.

8. See Filmography.

9. *Casablanca.* Everyone's favorite classic film. Orry-Kelly designed the deceptively simple costumes. See Filmography.

10. *Blood and Sand.* 1941 remake of Valentino's classic. See Filmography. Costumes designed by Jean Louis. In a legendary fashion partnership, *a la* Givenchy and Audrey Hepburn, Louis was largely responsible for creating Hayworth's mega-watt glamour image.

11. *Mask of Zorro*. Another remake of a Valentino classic. See Filmography.

12. See Filmography.

13. Song title: *Baby, Don't Get Hooked On Me* (1972). Words and music by Mac Davis.

14. Song title: *By the Time I Get To Phoenix* (1967). Words and music by Jimmy Webb.

15. Song title: *I've Got A New Attitude* (1985). Words and music by Sharon Robinson, Jonathan Gilutin, Bunny Hill.

16. See Filmography.

17. Jean-Yves Tadie. *Marcel Proust: A Life*. Viking. New York (2000).

18. See Filmography.

19. *Burberrys: An Elementary History of a Great Tradition*. Burberrys Limited. London.

20. *Ibid.*

21. *Ibid.*

22. *Lord and Lady Devereaux Milbank* and *Arthur Colin Milbank* are fictitious names. The inscription on the gravestone is factual.

23. See Filmography.

24. See Filmography.

25. See Filmography. Bonnie Cashin's remarkable costumes for this classic *film noir* are truly timeless. I've tracked this film for years, and her designs were wearable in 1980, perfect in 1990, and are beautifully wearable today.

26. *Vogue*. February, 2000, p. 164.

27. *Chanel, Chanel*: a film by Eli Hershon and Roberto Guerra.Writer/editor, Richard Howarth. (1986) Home Vision. Concord, Mass. A film using archival footage to chronicle the career and life of the great designer. Includes rare personal interviews with Madam Chanel herself.

28. Song title: *The Look of Love*. (1967). Words and music by Burt Bacharach and Hal David.

29. James Laver. *The Book of Public School, Old Boys, University, Army, Navy, Air   Force and Club TIES*. Seeley Service and Co. Ltd., pp. 27,28 (from the archives of Western Costume, Hollywood).

30. See Filmography

31. Diana Vreeland. *D.V.* Alfred A. Knopf. New York (1984), p. 163.

32. *The Red Shoes*. An exquisite film based on the Hans Christian Andersen story. See Filmography.

33. Robert San Souci, *The Red Heels*. Dial Books. New York (1996), p.6.

34. *Ibid.*, p.6.

35. Hans Christian Andersen. *The Little Mermaid and Other Fairy Tales*. Viking New York (1998), p. 49

36. See Filmography.

37. See Filmography.

38. See Filmography.

39. See Filmography.

40. See Filmography.

41. See Filmography.

42. See Filmography.

43. See Filmography.

44. See Filmography.

45. Based on comments by Marie Brenner, author of *Great Dames*. Television interview on the *Judith Regan Tonight* show. (February, 2000).

46. Song title: *"Diamonds Are A Girl's Best Friend."* (1949). Words by Leo Rubin, music by Jules Styne.

47. See Filmography.

48. Francois Truffaut. *Alfred Hitchcock*. Simon and Shuster, Inc. New York (1983), pp. 244-245.

49. *Ibid.*

50. *Ibid.*

51. Marion Van Offelen. *Nomads of Niger*. Harry N. Abrams, Inc. New York (1983)

…aver. *The Book of Public School, Old Boys,* …*sity, Army, Navy, Air Force and Club TIES,*

54. Diana Vreeland. *D.V.* Alfred A Knopf. New York (1984). pp. 127-129. Vreeland was the editor of both *Harper's Bazaar* and *Vogue*. Later, as Curator of Costume at New York's Metropolitan Museum, she developed the unique concept of museum fashion display as a real, razzle-dazzle Broadway-type show. If you truly love fashion, get acquainted with Diana in her autobiography, *D.V.*

55. *Ibid.*

56. *Ibid.*

57. *Vogue.* Feb. 2001. "The Many Faces of Yves," p. 535.

58. Alice Rawsthorn. *Yves Saint Laurent,* A Biography. Doubleday. New York (1996), p. 90.

59. *Mommie Dearest.* This movie is a treasure trove of authentic Forties and Fifties styles. See Filmography.

60. *Ibid.*

61. *"You Can Do It."* The interior design TV series starring the very engaging Christopher Lowell. (2001) 44 Blue Productions. Executive Producer: Christopher Lowell.

62. *In Style* magazine. February, 2000, pp.136-138.

63. *Ibid.*

64. *Ibid.*

65. Jeanine Basinger. *A Woman's View: How Hollywood Spoke to Woman — 1930/1960.* Alfred A. Knopf (1993), p. 245.

66. See Filmography.

67. See Filmography.

68. See Filmography

69. Jeanine Basinger. *A Woman's View. How Hollywood Spoke to Women.* p. 245

70. See Filmography.

71. See Filmography.

72. See Filmography.

73. Jeanine Basinger. *A Woman's View*, supra, p. 243

74. See footnote 46

75. See Filmography

76. See Filmography

77. See Filmography

78. See Filmography.

79. See Filmography

80. See Filmography

81. See Filmography

Bibliography

A Woman's View:
How Hollywood Spoke to Woman – 1930/1960
By Jeanine Basinger
Publisher: Alfred A. Knopf, (1993) New York

Burberrys:
An Elementary History of a Great Tradition
Publisher: Burberrys, Ltd., London

Christian Dior:
The Man Who Made the World Look New
By Marie-France Pochna.
Publisher: Arcade Publishing, (1996) New York

Chanel:
Her Style and Her Life
By Janet Wallach
Publisher: Doubleday, (1998) New York

Chanel:
A Woman of Her Own
By Axel Madsen
Publisher: H. Holt, (1990) New York

D.V.
By Diana Vreeland
Publisher: Alfred A. Knopf, (1984) New York

Four Hundred Years of Fashion
Editor: Natalie Rothstein
Published by The Victoria and Albert Museum,
London

Garde-robes:
Intimités Dévoilées, De Cléo De Mérode À.
Published by Musée de la Mode et du Textile,
(2000) Paris

Great Dames:
What I Learned From Older Women
By Marie Brenner
Publisher: Crown, (2000) New York

Hats, A History of Fashion in Headwear
By Hilda Amphlett
Publisher: Richard Sadler

Hitchcock
The Definitive Study of Alfred Hitchcock
By Francois Truffault
Publisher: Simon & Schuster, (1984) New York

The Little Mermaid and Other Fairy Tales
By Hans Christian Andersen
Collected and with introduction by Neil Phillip
Publisher: Viking, (1998) New York

Marion Davies: A Biography
By Fred Lawrence Guiles
Publisher: McGraw-Hill, (1972) New York

Modesty in Dress:
An Inquiry Into The Fundamentals of Fashion
By James Laver
Publisher: Heinemann
[Archives of Western Costume, Hollywood]

Movie Star:
A Look at the Women Who Made Hollywood
By Ethan Mordden
Publisher: St. Martin's Press, (1993) New York

Nomads of Niger
By Marion Van Offelen
Photography by Carol Beckwith
Published by Harry N. Abrams, Inc.
(1983) New York

The Red Heels
By Robert D. San Souci
Published by Dial Books, (1996) New York

Simply Halston:
The Untold Story
By Steven Gaines
Publisher: G.P. Putnam's Sons, (1991) New York

The Book of Public School, Old Boys, University,
Navy, Army, Air Force, and Club TIES
By James Laver
Publisher: Seeley Service and Co., Ltd.
[Archives of Western Costume, Hollywood]

20,000 Years of Fashion:
The History of Costume and Personal Adornment
By Francois Boucher
Publisher: Harry N. Abrams, Inc.,
(1987) New York

Yves Saint Laurent, A Biography
By Alice Rawsthorn
Published by Doubleday, (1996) New York

Filmography

Almost all of the films discussed in this book are available at the larger video rental stores. Viewing them will give you an expanded awareness of the influence of costume in the human drama, both on-screen and off. More than that, you'll have the opportunity to experience, once again, the enchantment of fabulous movie fashions. (Crank up the VCR!)

All About Eve (1950)
> Starring: Bette Davis, Gary Merrill
> Director: Joseph L. Mankiewicz

American Gigolo (1980)
> Starring: Richard Gere, Lauren Hutton
> Director: Paul Schrader
> Producer: Jerry Bruckheimer

Anna Christie (1930)
> Starring: Greta Garbo. Charles Bickford
> Director: Clarence Brown

Blood and Sand (1941)
Starring: Rita Hayworth, Tyrone Power
Director: Rouben Mamoulian
Producer: Darryl F. Zanuck

Breakfast at Tiffany's (1961)
Starring: Audrey Hepburn, George Peppard
Director: Blake Edwards
Producer: Martin Jurow, Richard Shepherd

Bugsy (1991)
Starring: Warren Beatty, Annette Benning
Director: Barry Levinson
Producers: Barry Levinson, Mark Johnson, Warren Beatty

Cabaret (1972)
Starring: Liza Minelli, Michael York
Director: Bob Fosse
Produced by Allied Artists

Casablanca (1942)
Starring: Ingrid Bergman, Humphrey Bogart
Director: Michael Curtiz
Produced by Warner Bros.

Cover Girl (1944)
Starring: Rita Hayworth, Gene Kelly
Director: Charles Vidor
Producer: Arthur Schwartz

Crossroads (2002)
    Starring: Britney Spears
    Director: Tamara Davis
    Produced by Filmco Enterprises

The Enchanted Cottage (1945)
    Starring: Dorothy McGuire, Robert Young
    Director: John Cromwell

Enchantment (1948)
    Starring: Teresa Wright, David Niven
    Director: Irving Reis

The English Patient (1996)
    Starring: Ralph Fiennes, Kristin Scott-Thomas
    Director: Anthony Minghella
    Producer: Saul Zaentz

Erin Brockovich (2000)
    Starring: Julia Roberts
    Director: Steven Soderbergh
    Producers: Danny DeVito, Michael Shamberg, Stacy Sher

It Happened One Night (1934)
    Starring: Clark Gable, Claudette Colbert
    Director: Frank Capra
    Producer: Harry Cohn

Laura (1944)
> Starring: Gene Tierney, Dana Andrews
> Producer/Director: Otto Preminger

The Mask of Zorro (1998)
> Starring: Catherine Zeta-Jones, Anthony Banderas
> Director: Martin Campbell

The Mexican (2001)
> Starring: Julia Roberts, Brad Pitt
> Director: Gore Verbinski
> Producers: John Baldecchi, Lawrence Bender

Mommie Dearest (1981)
> Starring: Faye Dunaway
> Director: Frank Perry
> Producer: Frank Yablans

Ninotchka (1939)
> Starring: Greta Garbo, Melvyn Douglas
> Director: Ernst Lubitsch

Notting Hill (1999)
> Starring: Julia Roberts, Hugh Grant
> Director: Roger Michell:

102 Dalmations (2000)
> Starring: Glenn Close
> Director: Kevin Lima
> Producer: Edward S. Feldman

Our Dancing Daughters (1928)
Starring: Joan Crawford, Johnny Mack Brown
Director: Harry Beaumont
Produced by MGM

Rear Window (1954)
Starring: Grace Kelly, James Stewart
Producer/Director: Alfred Hitchcock

Rebecca (1940)
Starring: Joan Fontaine, Lawrence Olivier
Director: Alfred Hitchcock
Producer: David O. Selznick

The Red Shoes (1948)
Starring: Moira Shearer, Anton Walbrook
Dierector: Michael Powell:
Producer: J. Arthur Rank

Sabrina (1954)
Starring: Audrey Hepburn, William Holden
Producer/Director: Billie Wilder

Secret Beyond the Door (1948)
Starring: Joan Bennett, Michael Redgrave
Director: Fritz Lang

Shanghai Express (1932)
Starring: Marlene Dietrich, Clive Brook
Producer/Director: Josef von Sternberg

Singin' In the Rain (1952)
Starring: Debbie Reynolds, Gene Kelly
Directors: Gene Kelly/Stanley Donen
Producer: Arthur Freed

Summertime (1955)
Starring: Katherine Hepburn, Rossano Brazzi
Director: David Lean
Produced by Lopert Films

The Swan (1956)
Starring: Grace Kelly, Louis Jourdan
Director: Charles Vidor

The Way We Were (1973)
Starring: Barbra Streisand, Robert Redford
Director: Syndey Pollack
Producer: Ray Stark

To Catch a Thief (1955)
Starring: Grace Kelly, Cary Grant
Producer/Director: Alfred Hitchcock

Two for the Road (1967)
Starring: Audrey Hepburn, Albert Finney
Producer/Director: Stanley Donen

Vertigo (1958)
Starring: Kim Novak, James Stewart
Producer/Director: Alfred Hitchcock

***Waterloo Bridge* (1940)**
　　Starring: Vivian Leigh, Robert Taylor
　　Director: Mervyn Le Roy
　　Producer: Sidney Franklin

About the Author

You can contact Gloria Heidi
on the internet at email address:
clpgroup@earthlink.net

About the Author

Best selling author (*Winning the Age Game*) and television personality, Gloria Heidi is recognized as one of the country's leading experts on the power and implication of personal image.

Her techniques of Image Dynamics™ have been featured in numerous major magazines, including

Cosmopolitan, People and *Family Circle*. Articles by and about Heidi have appeared in newspapers throughout the U.S., the U.K., Canada, Australia, Japan, and South America. She has lectured internationally and taught Image Dynamics™ at the University of California, Los Angeles and Berkeley campuses.

Heidi's know-how (plus her engaging personality) have made her a favorite guest expert on television talk shows from coast to coast, including Oprah and The Regis and Kathy Lee Show. As spokesperson for Clairol over a period of thirteen years, she established the TV Makeover as a staple of daytime television.

Heidi's expertise and unique approach to the subjects of image, fashion and beauty are the result of a rich background rooted in the magic of Hollywood imagery. She studied Costume for Film with legendary designer Edith Head (winner of eight Academy Awards) and has worked in front of and behind the camera. She appeared in fifty television commercials, was news anchor on a CBS affiliate, and hosted a daytime TV talk show. She has produced several hour long TV fashion spectaculars and beauty news features in Paris. Her documentary *Image: Projections of Identity* (written and produced by Heidi) was shown nationally on PBS.

In the world of fashion, she has worked as a freelance designer and as media consultant to international beauty firms, including *Parfums Givenchy*, Paris.

Heidi divides her time between California's Marin County and Paris.

Quick Order Form

TUDOR-HALL PRESS

Fax orders: (866) 583-1376. Send this form.

Phone orders: (877) 235-9700

Email orders: cplgroup@earthlink.net

Postal orders: Tudor-Hall Press, 336 Bon Air Center, #136
Greenbrae, CA 94904

Please send the following:

# of Copies	Unit Price	Amount
_____ *Hang-Ups!*	$13.95	_____
_____ *Close-Up*	$15.95	_____
_____ *Face-Up!*	$29.95	_____
Gloria Heidi's "Winning The Age Game" **Special Reports**	Free List	_____
**Add shipping and handling:		$ 4.05
*Sales Tax:		_____

*Please add 7.5% for products shipped to California addresses.

** International: Shipped by air.
    Add $5.00 additional S&H for each book ordered.

TOTAL AMOUNT ENCLOSED: _____
[checks or money orders]

Name: _____

Address: _____

City: _____ State: _____ Zip: _____

Telephone: _____ Email: _____

Close-Up: Gloria Heidi's 10-Day Makeover Program
    Critics call it: *"The best beauty book I have ever read"*

Face-Up!: Gloria Heidi's Easy Exercise System to Firm,
    Tone & Recontour Your Face
"I see a subtle, wonderful difference — it works!" S.A., Virginia